How To Get To Heaven

By: Robert Sales

Copyright © 2009 by Robert Sales

How To Get To Heaven
by Robert Sales

Printed in the United States of America

ISBN 978-1-60791-232-3

All rights reserved solely by the author. The author guarantees all contents are original and do not infringe upon the legal rights of any other person or work. No part of this book may be reproduced in any form without the permission of the author. The views expressed in this book are not necessarily those of the publisher.

Unless otherwise indicated, Bible quotations are taken from The *Holy Bible, New International Version* ®, NIV, Copyright © 1973, 1978, 1984 by International Bible Society, Used by permission of Zondervan, and The Holy Bible, *New Living Translation,* NLT, Copyright © 1996, 2004, Used by permission of Tyndale house Publishers, Inc., Wheaton, Illinois 60189, and *The Message,* Copyright © 1993, 1994, 1995, 1996, 2000, 2001, 2002, Used by permission of NavPress Publishing Group, and The New Century Version, NCV, Copyright © 2005 by Thomas Nelson, Inc., and *The Living Bible:* Tyndale House, 1997, Copyright © 1971 by Tyndale House Publishers, Inc., and The *New King James Version,* NKJV, Copyright © 1982 by Thomas Nelson, Inc., Used by permission.

And When I Die
Words and Music by Laura Nyro
Copyright © 1966 (Renewed 1994) EMI BLACKWOOD MUSIC INC.

www.xulonpress.com

Dedication

To my hero – Kimberly Kay

and

To my Dad, who was one of the main reasons I wrote this book.

"See you soon Dad!"

Table of Contents

Chapter 1	Preparing The Way	9
Chapter 2	Who Is God?	19
Chapter 3	Who Am I?	37
Chapter 4	Selection Criteria	51
Chapter 5	Judgment Day	63
Chapter 6	Your Choice	79
Chapter 7	Heaven	87
Chapter 8	Hell	107
Chapter 9	What Now?	119

Chapter 1

Preparing The Way

When you ask most people if they want to go to Heaven, the overwhelming response is "Yes." It's almost as if they are saying – "But of course, where else would anyone want to go?" However, most of these responses don't have the sense of confidence that communicates that they KNOW they are actually going to make it into Heaven. Most are just hoping that Heaven is where they will end up when all is said and done, without understanding what God requires of us in order to get into Heaven.

Interestingly enough, most people don't put much thought behind what is the most important decision of their lives. And why is that? After all, we spend a significant amount of time and energy when making decisions concerning such things as marriage, jobs, cars, and homes. And yet all of those decisions involve matters that are of incredibly short duration in light of eternity, which is what the choice of making sure you end up in Heaven is all about. There are some compelling reasons for this lack of attention when it comes to the topic of Heaven and life after death. After some honest reflection, we can all relate and admit to the main underlying reasons we procrastinate are: *the fear of death and the unknown, ignorance, no real sense of urgency, and life's busyness.*

But the first question that needs to be asked is not so much how do we get to Heaven, but what is Heaven really all about? Where is it? What's it going to be like? Who's going to be there? Before examining what Heaven is like, we need to understand what God intends Heaven to be. Only then can we come to the point of deciding whether we really want to spend eternity there. Quite naturally, the things we think about most when we think about Heaven itself are its physical attributes – pearly gates, street of gold, mansions, and the like. While these all describe the physical part of Heaven, they fall short of understanding what Heaven really is all about. If you think about it, describing Heaven in these physical terms would be like restricting a description of someone to the clothing they are wearing.

Fortunately, we don't have to guess what Heaven will be all about. God tells us what we need to know. Reflecting on our lives, everything we cherish is rooted in our shared relationships and their respective experiences and memories. Likewise, the real substance of Heaven is rooted in the people who will be there and the relationships we will have with one another. The most important relationship you will have in Heaven will be the one with God Himself. In light of this, it's interesting how so many people live their entire lives avoiding God, and yet insist that they want to spend an eternity with Him.

So, let's think a little about Heaven here. Is it just a cleaned-up version of what we have here on Earth? Is it a utopia? Most of us would say that Heaven has to be at least a far better place than anything humanity has ever known, both in terms of relationships and our surroundings. So what does God tell us about Heaven? He tells us that Heaven is a perfect place, where there will be no more pain, tears, or death. And how can that be without coming to the realization that the design of Heaven centers on perfect and eternal relationships? The more we reflect on Heaven in those terms, the more exciting it becomes – a place we can look forward to calling home. At the same time, we pause and wonder how that could ever come to pass.

So where is this place called Heaven? Does it exist now, or is it something that is yet to come? The answer is "Yes!" There is a place we call Heaven that currently exists, and one that is going to be the final and perfected Heaven – or as God calls it, "the new Heaven and new Earth." In fact, understanding life as it currently exists and how it will ultimately be for eternity is not exclusively reserved for Heaven as our ultimate destination. Life gives us incredible insight into the only other option for eternity – Hell, or what is more accurately called the Lake of Fire.

This book is going to provoke you to think "outside the box" of commonly held conceptions and misconceptions about Heaven. Many of these conceptions and misconceptions come from our exposure to various sources such as movies, teachings, conversations with others, imagination, and books. It's interesting that some people claim you have to disengage your brain if you believe in God and Heaven. The reality is that God wants us to use that very organ to begin understanding Him and Heaven, especially as they relate to us individually. To get this thinking process in motion, let us consider some "statements" God makes about Heaven:

- Heaven is a very special place that only perfect people can enter. (*Now don't panic or give up, because there is great news on how God can make us all perfect.*)

"Nothing impure will ever enter (heaven), nor will anyone who does what is shameful or deceitful, but only those whose names are written in the Lamb's book of life." Rev 21:27 NIV

- Heaven is the only place where God and mankind can have a full and complete relationship with Him and others the way He intended it to be from the beginning.

"the LORD God formed the man from the dust of the ground and breathed into his nostrils the breath of life, and the man became a living being" Gen 2:7 NIV

"Then the man and his wife heard the sound of the LORD God as he was walking in the garden in the cool of the day, and they hid from the LORD God among the trees of the garden." Gen 3:8 NIV

"And I heard a loud voice from the throne saying, "Now the dwelling of God is with men, and he will live with them. They will be his people, and God himself will be with them and be their God." Rev 21:31 NIV

- Living life as a "good person" doesn't get anyone into Heaven. No amount of good works or good thoughts qualifies you to get into Heaven.

"For it is by grace you have been saved, through faith—and this not from yourselves, it is the gift of God" Eph 2:8 NIV

- Religion or being religious does NOT get you into Heaven. In fact, it may be the very thing that keeps you out!

"You are Israel's teacher," said Jesus, "and do you not understand these things?" John 3:10 NIV

- God makes it possible for everyone everywhere to get into Heaven, no matter where they live or how many "bad things" they may have done.

"For God so loved the world that he gave his one and only Son, that whoever believes in him shall not perish but have eternal life." John 3:16 NIV

- Not everyone wants to go to Heaven, even though that is God's desire.

"But because of your stubbornness and your unrepentant heart, you are storing up wrath against yourself for the day of God's wrath, when his righteous judgment will be revealed." Romans 2:5 NIV

"The Lord is not slow in keeping his promise, as some understand slowness. He is patient with you, not wanting anyone

to perish, but everyone to come to repentance." 2 Peter 3:9 NIV

- There is also a real place called Hell, which just happens to be the only alternate destination reserved for those who reject God's way of getting into Heaven.

"Then he will say to those on his left, 'Depart from me, you who are cursed, into the eternal fire prepared for the devil and his angels." Matt 25:41 NIV

You may be surprised that one of the "statements" here is the one where God tells us that religion or being religious not only doesn't get you into Heaven, but it may disqualify you altogether. At first glance, that seems contradictory. First of all, it's important to note that this book is not about discrediting or endorsing any religion – it's about the good news that everyone has the opportunity to get into Heaven and has nothing to do with religion. It is solely based on what has to happen between you and God. When we examine the many religions, we see a very common theme that validates many points God brings to light. The most obvious purpose almost all religions have is recognizing the spiritual side of our existence and our need to seek God. So it is most unfortunate when people state that their religion is better than anyone else's. The ultimate goal of most religions is to draw close to God and spend eternity with Him. What God tells us is that there is only one way that can happen. It's not based on what any man or religion mandates, it's what God says. By the time you complete this book, you will have a better understanding of what God's plan is for you to spend eternity with Him and others in perfect harmony.

The important thing to come to terms with here about religion is that God never established any religion; they are all exclusively man-made institutions. Therefore, we must realize is that getting into Heaven is not subject to any religious system. Man-made institutions by nature are defective. The point has been brought up that being religious may be the biggest obstacle to getting into Heaven. I think we can better relate to this statement by reflecting on the type of people who flaunt themselves as being religious. They have an air of being better than you are; they judge you and treat you almost with contempt, implying they have it all together. These very religious, pious behaviors are as ungodly as it gets. It's no wonder people run from some religions because of people who live in such an ungodly manner.

Don't misunderstand what I am trying to say here. Religion may help people seek God, but history shows time and again that it has a strong tendency to focus on the observance of rules and regulations, instead of being the means of having a relationship with God. Religion in and of itself can alienate you from God instead of drawing you closer to Him, because the focus can be more of following the rules rather than focusing in on God. The thinking becomes, *if I follow the "rules" I will be "right" with God.* The acts of following the rules themselves are dead and meaningless; it's the relationship that brings you to life. If all we have to do is behave (act) religiously our entire lives to get into Heaven, you don't need God to get there, you are trying to do it on your own personal merit. What God will say to the people who are strictly religious is: "I never knew you!", and then deny them entrance into His heavenly kingdom. Needless to say, there will be many surprised people on the Day of Judgment.

It is not enough to just have a strong desire to get into Heaven. You have to understand what God says is essential for that to happen – God does not make any exceptions. When people share what they discovered God requires, many people say that is narrow-minded. God says the road to Heaven is indeed a narrow road.

This book provides you with all the information you need to make your own choice about where you want spend eternity. It is the navigational roadmap to Heaven not found on any electronic mapping system.

Here is an outline of what you can look forward to reading:

Chapter 2 Who is God? – The starting point has to be God. Knowing Him makes everything we need to know about Heaven much clearer. What you will discover is the more you know God, the more you want to know Him. As a result, you will come to realize all He wants is the best for you. He's all about true love and giving. He wants to have a personal relationship with you now, so you can have a full and eternal one with Him in Heaven. You will "see" the difference between God as He reveals Himself to us now, and how that will change once we get to Heaven.

Chapter 3 Who am I? – The next most relevant part of Heaven is you. It is important that you come to know yourself and your purpose while here on Earth, and your destiny as God intends. You will discover you are an eternal being who will live forever. You will come to see yourself in a new light as a person who is responsible to make decisions – each one having its own consequences. Your most important decision is the one of where you choose to spend eternity, based on God's plan. This chapter will also help you come to terms with the fact that you can't get to Heaven on your own because of your shortcomings.

Chapter 4 Selection Criteria – If there is one thing that God makes crystal clear to us, it is the unchanging fact that people get into Heaven only by the path God has laid out. He makes no compromises or exceptions. These criteria or requirements are what qualify us to enter into a perfect relationship with God for an eternity in Heaven. There is no other way that this can happen, or He would have told us. These criteria are so specific (yet simple) that anything short of them will fail to get you into Heaven. We will learn in this chapter what these criteria are, why God has put them into place, and just how simple He has made it for us. Here too, we will read the story of a man who rejected God during his lifetime that condemned him to Hell. Once there, in his state of utter misery, he desperately wanted to warn his family not to make the same mistake.

Chapter 5 Judgment Day – For some reason, we all seem to instinctively know that this day is coming. If there ever has been a subject man is fascinated with, it is about a specific "day" where every person will be judged for what he or she did during their lifetime. Yet this day will be quite different than most imagine it to be. This is the day when God will separate those who will go to Heaven from those who will be separated from Him for all eternity in the Lake of Fire. Which destination each person goes to is based on the choice we make during our lifetime regarding God's invitation to be reconciled with Him, and starting that relationship while on Earth. The details in this chapter on what happens this fateful day will surprise you and hopefully guide you to seek God now, instead of discovering what a terrible mistake you made by misunderstanding what this day really is all about.

Chapter 6   Your Choice – God made each person a free will being – He lets us make choices every day. Life is a series of decisions. Some more impacting than others. If there ever was a single most important decision in our lives, it is choosing where you will live for all eternity. God will not force you to love Him and spend eternity with Him. However, He definitely influences us through our relationships and circumstances to look to Him and cry out to Him. The beauty and simplicity of God's design for being reconciled to Him and deciding to have this relationship will amaze you. If there ever was a "too good to be true" story, this is it. Yet it is true. We will visit the consequences of a decision for or against accepting God's gift.

Chapter 7   Heaven – What God tells us about Heaven is enough to both entice and challenge you! In His description of Heaven, He tells us about its exclusivity and perfection that actually defies description. It is the perfect setting for perfect relationships, joy, peace, and a real sense of family, belonging, and purpose. Not only will it be a perfect "place," but also it is where relationships reach their full potential without any of the conflicts we face here on Earth. Can you even begin to imagine not having any arguments, jealousies, envy, or strife? One has to wonder why anyone would want to choose any place else as their future eternal residence. We will come to understand the difference between Heaven as it currently exists, and what the New Heaven will be like.

Chapter 8 Hell – This is the only other alternative to Heaven. As wonderful and indescribable as Heaven is, the opposite extremes apply to Hell – "darkest darkness," "unquenchable thirst," and "a place where the fire never goes out," are only a few of the descriptions God uses, relative to the desolation of Hell. Just reading about Hell should scare anyone who does not think they want to go to Heaven into reconsidering. The most sobering and departing thought here is that once there, there is no turning back – it is an eternal decision. And as devastating as Hell is as it currently exists, it actually gets worse when Hell itself is tossed into the Lake of Fire, forever sealing the fate of those who reject God's rescuing hand.

Chapter 9 What Now? – Here we face the decision of accepting or rejecting God's way into Heaven. Everyone who chooses to reach out and touch God's hand, accepting His gift of an eternal relationship with Him, will discover that life will never be the same. Guaranteed!! Yet, it does not end at this point of decision, it's actually a new beginning. Along with this new life come new responsibilities. You will discover what God requires of your new relationship with Him and how you can develop and deepen it, so much so that you will want to share this newfound joy with others. For those who still reject God's gift, we will again revisit the full consequences of that decision and offer a sincere prayer that your heart will change before it is indeed too late.

I hope by now your appetite has been stimulated to the point of wanting to read on with an open heart and mind. Ask God to help you eliminate anything that will block the truth out as you read this book. Hopefully, you will discover that God and His gift are what have been missing in your life. That empty feeling way down deep will go away.

Chapter 2

Who Is God?

—∾—

"Who is God?" There is no greater question we can ask ourselves. Once we discover the answer, we can begin to understand the meaning of everything else in its proper place and perspective. The very meaning and purpose of our lives will come into focus once we know God. So who is God?

- God is Spirit, holy, perfect, eternal, infinite, and personal.
- He is all-powerful, all-knowing, and ever-present.
- He is the giver of life, our creator, provider, protector, healer, and helper in time of need.
- He is faithful, trustworthy, truthful, just, patient, kind, good, gentle, peaceful, and wise.
- He is loving, forgiving, gracious.
- He is Immanuel (God with us), and if we believe, our redeemer/savior/Messiah/the anointed one, our Father.
- And finally, He is our Judge.

The only way we will come to know God as just described, is if we take the time to seek and find Him. When we don't know God, He seems far away, disinterested in us, and maybe we even think that He may not exist. We may feel that God is too busy to be bothered with us as individuals. Nothing can be further from the truth.

God loves us more than we could ever imagine, no matter what we may have done.

So, how do we get to know someone we have never seen, can't touch or feel, or have any idea of where He is or how to get in touch with Him? The task of getting to know God would be daunting and overwhelming if He had not given us the ability to know Him.

What we can be sure of is that God designed each one of us to be able to understand all we need to know to have a personal relationship with Him now, and ultimately in Heaven.

God has made it possible for us to get to know Him in a threefold way:

- Instinctively
- Evidenced by our surroundings
- Speaking to us through others and directly to us

To make sure no one ever misses out on knowing Him, God implanted the knowledge of His existence in every human being. This knowledge is as much a part of everyone as their physical DNA – you could say it's in our "spiritual DNA." Although the evidence of God's existence is all around us, unless we take the time to notice Him, we will miss the obvious. It's like when we move about, nothing we see registers specifically unless we consciously pause and observe what is around us.

No matter where you live, what culture you come from, what your standing in life might be, what your physical limitations might be, what religion you belong to, the evidence of God's existence is all around us every day. God made sure not one person would be unable to know Him or be dependent on others to get to know Him. This is what God tells us about that innate knowledge:

"The truth about God is known to [everyone] instinctively; God has put this knowledge in their hearts. ….. So they will have no excuse [when they stand before God at Judgment Day]." Romans 1:19-20 TLB

God also gives us affirming evidence of His existence from our surroundings, reinforcing what we know instinctively:

"The heavens declare the glory of God; the skies proclaim the work of his hands. Day after day they pour forth speech; night after night they display knowledge. There is no speech or language where their voice is not heard. Their voice goes out into all the earth, their words to the ends of the world." Psalm 19:1-4 NIV

Since the vast majority of who God is goes beyond what we can fully understand, we need to start our search by "seeing" God from the following perspectives:

- God alone – Before anything else existed
- God in light of the past
- God in light of today
- God in light of the future

To start with, we are going to begin our search by trying to know Him outside of the known Universe. This is very unfamiliar, definitely challenging territory, but a very necessary part of understanding God.

God Alone - Before Anything Else Existed

God is not in the least bit limited or constrained by what we know as the physical realm – the Universe. When we try to see God outside the known Universe, we need to realize that God existed before anything else. He is the one who brought everything into existence. Some argue that God must have had a beginning, but that would mean He was limited by the very thing He created – including time. In reality, we can never come to the point of truly understanding how there could ever be someone who never had a beginning, since our very existence is limited to the realm of time. This is where we have to begin to trust what God tells us.

To understand how God can exist outside of the Universe, we need to go back before all time, before even the very beginning. God identifies Himself in such a way that communicates that He simply is:

"I AM WHO I AM" Exodus 3:14 NIV

Simply, God is who He is. God never had a beginning, He always was, and always will be. Now we need to think about God's being, His substance. In order for God to exist outside the physical realm, God has to have His being as something other than the physical. Once again, God helps us to understand that dimension of who He is by telling us:

"[I AM] sheer being itself — Spirit" John 4:24 The Message

God is a real living being without any of the limitations we are bound by. Not having any limitations tell us that He is absolutely and completely perfect. He tells us plainly:

"... [I AM] perfect." Matthew 5:48 NIV

So what exactly does it mean to be perfect, and why should that matter to us? The Merriam-Webster dictionary defines perfect as: *"being entirely without fault or defect: flawless; satisfying all requirements."* It is essential that God be perfect. Anything less would mean that God is lacking something and would need to draw on something other than Himself to continue existing.

Coming at perfection from the personal side of God, the Merriam-Webster dictionary further defines God as: *"the Being perfect in power, wisdom, and goodness..."* God knows everything there is to know; He sees everything without the limit of space and time; He is all-powerful; He is not limited in any way. He doesn't need to improve in any capacity, because He is totally complete. God lacks nothing.

Being perfect also means that God is unchanging by sheer implication, otherwise that would mean God has room for improvement. God affirms this characteristic:

"I the Lord do not change." Malachi 3:6 NIV

God knows us beyond what we know about ourselves, and therefore says the same thing in many ways – ways in which we can better understand. So in order for us to get to know Him in this regard, He further frames Himself as unchanging within the context of space and time:

"[I AM] the same yesterday and today and forever." Hebrews 13:8 NIV

In a real sense, being unchanging or continuously the same makes Him very predictable as well as dependable. Some would jump to the conclusion that this would make Him vulnerable, when indeed it is one of His strong points, as this stability allows us to know Him without being concerned about who He might be tomorrow.

Perfection and being unchanging go hand-in-hand, but it also leads us to another characteristic that God reveals about Himself. God's very essence is that He is pure, without defect, and untainted. God uses a term to capture this dimension of who He is:

"[I AM] holy" Leviticus 19:2 NIV

God being perfect, unchanging and holy is vital to having a relationship with Him. Having a full and complete relationship with God can only be realized to its fullness if the other individual is equally holy and perfect. Since we are neither holy nor perfect, there is no way any person could ever have that type of relationship with God. But there is great news, as we will see, as God made a way for that relationship to take place.

This is an extremely brief overview of trying to "see" and understand that God exists apart from anything else. He is who He is, no matter what. We will now move back into familiar territory, the realm of the Universe where we can see God in light of the past, the present and the future.

God In Light Of The Past

It is easier for us to understand God when we see Him from a historical standpoint. Our history has a beginning, and so we will start there so we don't miss how God related and interacted with creation and mankind from that perspective.

Many of the theories and speculation people have come up with over the ages may sound reasonable, but they are exactly that - theories and speculation. How much faith does it take to believe an individual or group of individuals who, many millennia later, try to recount with certainty what happened at the beginning of time? Why should we trust anyone other than the one who was there? If we are to trust anyone, God would surely be the best choice.

God may not be visible to us, but He knows exactly how to communicate with us so that we can get to know Him personally.

"In the past God spoke to our forefathers through the prophets at many times and in various ways" Hebrews 1:1NIV

God did not on a whim decide to create something. As we just read, God is perfect and has everything necessary to create. He has within Himself all knowledge, wisdom and power to do anything that conforms to His character. Before He launched creation, God planned and designed every detail based on His divine purpose. Being a creative creator is a natural outpouring of who He is. He is in a real sense a perfectionist, as reflected in what He created, from the very smallest detail to the splendor of its enormity. Putting creation in motion required a plan. He tells us:

"From the very beginning [I] decided this in keeping with [my] plan." Ephesians 1:11 NCV

Everything God created was perfect, intertwined and worked together for His unified plan. This included our very own planet Earth:

"This is my plan for the whole earth-I will do it by my mighty power that reaches everywhere around the world." Isa 14:26 TLB

God created all things – the entire Universe and all that is in it, both the visible and the invisible. The invisible is not just the material side, but it also includes the spiritual realm. So there would be no doubt about what happened at the beginning, God gave us a firsthand account of what happened, as recorded in the first two chapters of Genesis. First, we will visit what God tells us about how the Universe came into being:

"In the beginning [I] created the heavens and the earth." Genesis 1:1 NIV

Since God existed before anything else, it is logical and reasonable to attribute all of creation to God alone. But we don't have to rely on our own reasoning, as God tells us:

"I am the Lord, who has made all things, who alone stretched out the heavens, who spread out the earth by myself" Isaiah 44:24 NIV

His workmanship is a divine signature, much like an artist who signs his or her canvas.

"The heavens declare the glory of God; the skies proclaim the work of his hands." Psalm 19:1 NIV

Even the purposes of His creation begin to surface when we stop and take notice. God's role as designer merges with His plans and eternal purposes. One of the biggest obstacles to knowing God is attributing what He has done to someone else. This belief can be the ultimate slap in God's face. But He always leaves room for us while we are still breathing to come to full recognition and acceptance of who He is and what He has done.

God moved from creating the heavens and planet Earth to that of creating life itself, starting with vegetation, then the animal kingdom:

> *"And God said, "Let the land produce living creatures according to their kinds: livestock, creatures that move along the ground, and wild animals, each according to its kind." And it was so. Genesis 1:24 NIV*

This is where God's design of "according to its kind" gives man his first hint that there is a code we have come to know as DNA, embedded within each living organism. It can be called the blueprint of life. Bill Gates, founder of Microsoft, commented that, *"DNA is like a software program, only much more complex than anything we've ever devised."* Who would logically and credibly attribute such a complex and vital molecule to a mindless beginning? The mathematical probability of DNA coming together on its own is beyond ridiculous.

What God had created up to this point laid the foundation for what God was going to do next - create mankind. Here is what God tells us what happened next:

> *"Then God said, "Let us make man in our image, in our likeness, and let them rule over the fish of the sea and the birds of the air, over the livestock, over all the earth, and over all the creatures that move along the ground."" Genesis 1:26 NIV*

Unlike anything else God created to this point, He created mankind in His image and likeness. Since God is spirit, God is telling us that His image and likeness refers to our spiritual being. Here is how God created man in His likeness:

"Then the Lord God formed man from the dust of the ground and breathed into his nostrils the breath or spirit of life, and man became a living being." Genesis 2:7 NIV

Man was set apart from the rest of all creation, as God planned and designed. Man is unique in that he was created to have a personal, intimate relationship with God. Since God is personal, it means He is relational. He is involved with and cares for His creation.

As such, the first thing God did was prepare a place for Adam to live. God was like a Father to Adam, providing for him, caring and instructing him. He gave him responsibilities and instructed him on what he should and should not do.

Unfortunately, Adam and Eve both breached their trust with God, as we will see in the next chapter. This would have been the end of the story, except that God is a loving God – He is loving and forgiving. So much so that He promised to make a way for people to be reconciled to Him. God devised another plan; this time it was a promise of redemption. Keeping this promise was going to cost Him dearly – the biggest sacrifice anyone could ever make.

His plan was to bridge the gap of our imperfection with His perfection, making it possible once again to have a personal relationship with Him. Mankind lost its initial relationship with God through the choice made by one man. God would bring about this reconciliation through a man – the second Adam.

"The first man Adam became a living being; the last Adam, a life-giving spirit." 1 Corinthians 15:45 NIV

The second Adam was none other than God Himself taking on human form, something that was possible because man was truly made in His image to begin with. God called him the Anointed One/savior/Christ/Messiah. All the same terms for the same person. This is a statement that will cause many to draw back because of our preconceived notions, limitations of being able to understand what God can do, and teachings we received from others. The question then becomes: "Who are we that we think God is limited to what we can conceive?"

> "With man this is impossible, but not with God; all things are possible with God." Mark 10:27 NIV

Believing what God tells us about Jesus the Christ is the key to everything associated with anyone getting into Heaven. It is the single most important point of faith we have to exercise about what God tells us.

So where is the evidence that Jesus is actually God almighty? It actually starts at the very beginning when God said:

> "Let **us** make man in **our** image" Genesis 1:26 NIV

Notice that God said let **"US"** make man in **"OUR"** image. These words convey clearly that there is a plurality, or more than one being, within the identity of one God. That can only mean that God in a real sense is multi-dimensional, with a unity or singleness about Him. We have little problem understanding ourselves as having a body, soul, and spirit; and, we talk about a single object as having three dimensions all the time. For example an egg has three visible parts to it – the shell, the white and the yoke; in a less tangible yet understandable dimension is time – past, present, and future. Why then can't God have as part of His being dimensions that go beyond what we can conceive, let alone fully understand?

So just how did God come into this world as a human being? Did God give us any proofs or evidence of the fact that He would come and walk among us as a man? The proof starts with God talking through the prophets, foretelling of the evidence that would validate the One who was to come. There are literally dozens of these prophecies of Jesus being God and His coming. We will only address two of these: His virgin birth and how He would suffer and die.

Since God was coming into the world as a man, He chose to come the same way we all did, by being born of a woman. There was something very unique about how He was conceived in human form, in that He was born of a virgin:

> "Therefore the Lord himself will give you a sign: The virgin will be with child and will give birth to a son, and will call

him Immanuel which means, "God with us."" Isaiah 7:14 NIV

And so God came into the world:

"Today in the town of David a Savior has been born to you; he is Christ the Lord." Luke 2:11 NIV

He came for a specific purpose:

"For the Son of Man came to seek and to save what was lost." Luke 19:10 NIV

The impossible was unfolding into the possible, because God was the one bringing this to pass. He was coming as a man to save mankind from its fate of being separated from Him for all eternity. God does not expect us to fully understand how He could come into the world as a Human being:

"God, did not consider equality with [Himself] something to be grasped, but made himself nothing, taking the very nature of a servant, being made in human likeness." Philippians 2:6-7 NIV

What God does require of us is to have faith that what He is telling us is indeed the truth and nothing less. This is such a critical point of understanding who God is that Jesus, the Son of God, made the statement that whoever:

"rejects me rejects him who sent me." Luke 10:16 NIV

In other words, when anyone rejects Jesus as being God almighty, they are, in fact, rejecting God Himself.
But God did not expect us to exercise blind faith. He came down to Earth to be with us, instruct us more clearly – the ultimate proof. The religious leaders of the day had complicated what God had made so simple. The religious rulers made it impossible for people

to get to know God personally. That same challenge exists today, in that so many religions either believe or give the strong impression that it is by doing good deeds and being a good person that God will let people into Heaven. God is not interested in our good deeds to have a relationship with Him. He clarified that for us:

"For it is by grace you have been saved, through faith — and this not from yourselves, it is the gift of God— not by works, so that no one can boast." Ephesians 2:8-9 NIV

When Jesus taught, people immediately saw there was something different about Him. His teachings were validated by what He did and the authority by which He did them:

"All the people were amazed and said to each other, 'What is this teaching? With authority and power he gives orders to evil spirits and they come out!'" Luke 4:36 NIV

His authority extended beyond His words, in that the spiritual world was subjected to Him. Another instance that clearly demonstrated Jesus' authority was when Jesus was with His closest followers. They were in a boat in the Sea of Galilee, during a storm that was so bad they thought they were all going to die. Jesus' response to the situation:

"[Jesus] rebuked the wind and said to the waves, 'Quiet! Be still!' Then the wind died down and it was completely calm… They were terrified and asked each other, 'Who is this? Even the wind and the waves obey him!'" Mark 4:39-41 NIV

The guys who spent most of their time with Jesus were coming to the realization that He was more than just a man. Jesus was more than a good teacher, a prophet, and maybe a little more, and when asked, He told them. Jesus claimed to be God almighty. He spoke plainly:

"I and the Father are one." John 10:30 NIV

This claim was not only controversial, it was punishable by death in those days. Jesus did risk death when He was brought before the religious leaders of the day. Here is an excerpt from Jesus' "trial:"

"At daybreak the council of the elders of the people, both the chief priests and teachers of the law, met together, and Jesus was led before them. 'If you are the Christ,' they said, 'tell us.' Jesus answered, 'If I tell you, you will not believe me, and if I asked you, you would not answer. But from now on, the Son of Man will be seated at the right hand of the mighty God.' They all asked, 'Are you then the Son of God?" He replied, 'You are right in saying I AM.'" Luke 22:66-70 NIV

Shortly after this episode, Jesus was crucified and died. But it was no ordinary execution. It was one God orchestrated, and a death Jesus accepted willingly because He saw beyond the immediate pain He was suffering. He knew it was the only way anyone would ever be able to get into Heaven. But His death was only the first step. The ultimate proof of Jesus being God almighty was when He rose from the dead. Death could not hold Him, to the point where He now holds the key for all mankind.

Jesus told His disciples that He was going to be crucified. He also told them that He was going to come back from the dead.

"He said to them, 'The Son of Man is going to be betrayed into the hands of men. They will kill him, and on the third day he will be raised to life.'" Matthew 17:22-23 NIV

They saw the first part in harsh reality, but in their grief and humanity they were very slow to believe what He said would happen next – they were honestly skeptical. When word came that He had indeed come back to life, this doubt surfaced:

"When Jesus rose early on the first day of the week, he appeared first to Mary Magdalene ... She went and told those who had been with him and who were mourning and

weeping. When they heard that Jesus was alive and that she had seen him, they did not believe it." Mark 16:9-11 NIV

Many have been skeptical about all the claims Jesus made, but they are only having the same doubts some of His closest companions were having. Take the Apostle Thomas for instance – also known as Doubting Thomas. Thomas demanded proof positive before he would believe that Jesus was raised from the dead. Jesus gave him that proof, and this is how Thomas responded when Jesus appeared to him:

"'My Lord and my God!' Then Jesus told him, 'Because you have seen me, you have believed; blessed are those who have not seen and yet have believed.'" John 20:28-29 NIV

God is not subject to or limited by death. He was eternal and all-powerful then, and He remains eternal and all-powerful today. He never changes. That was then - what about today?

God In Light Of Today

God is as active today as He was at any time in history. Particularly, He is active in everything that is going on in our lives, whether or not we recognize it. What may be getting in our way of "seeing" God may be because our lives are so busy.

God is as accessible to one person as much as He is to the next. He may seem far away, distant, silent, untouchable, and maybe even unknowable. The amazing thing is, when we deliberately take the time to sincerely look for Him, we discover He is right there – within our reach. It's all a matter of the heart and taking the time to seek Him.

Knowing who God is, is the same for everyone no matter who we may be, where we live, how old we may be, what we look like, what religion we belong to, or anything else that makes us different from others. The fact is, God does not have favorites:

"There is no partiality with God." Romans 2:11 NKJV

His Plan included each one of us, as He knew everything about us even before we were created. So much so that:

"He determined the times set for [us] and the exact places where [we] should live. God did this so that [we] would seek him and perhaps reach out for him and find him, though he is not far from each one of us." Acts 17:26-28 NIV

All of this attention to detail is because God knows us so well and loves us so much that He extends that love in the hope that everyone may:

"... understand the greatness of Christ's love — how wide and how long and how high and how deep that love is. Christ's love is greater than anyone can ever know" Eph 3:18-19 NCV

People long to meet their "soul mate." To connect at all levels of a relationship filled with unconditional love. No one person can ever fulfill that desire except God. In reality, God is more than our soul mate, He is our spirit mate. He made a way for that connection to happen by what He did in the person of Jesus the Christ. He loves us more than anyone else ever could, and proved it by giving His all – paying the price we could never pay.

He did all He had to do to initiate a relationship with each one of us. But as with any relationship, it takes two to make it work. So:

"Today, if you hear his voice" Hebrews 3:7 NIV

We must not harden our hearts and turn away, because God is giving each one of us many opportunities to turn to Him. God proves this in these two accounts of individuals who had a change of heart, taking the initiative to have that relationship with Him. One took the time out of the routine of his day to seek God, and the other did it as he was about to take his last breath:

> "When Jesus reached the spot, he looked up and said to him, 'Zacchaeus, come down immediately. I must stay at your house today.' ... Jesus said to him, 'Today salvation has come to this house ...'" Luke 19:5, 9 NIV

And while Jesus was on the cross, the man next to him said:

> "'Jesus, remember me when you come into your kingdom.' Jesus answered him, 'I tell you the truth, today you will be with me in paradise.'" Luke 23:42-43 NIV

God is faithful – faithful to make sure each one of us has an opportunity to have a relationship with Him no matter when we live, where we live, what we may look like, what we do for a living or what religion we belong to.

God In Light Of The Future

At some point in time, God will bring everything as we know it to an end. God will reconcile every right and wrong done from the beginning of time. There will be new beginning where He sets everything in motion from that point going forward for all eternity.

Exactly when this will happen, only God knows for sure, but we are told that we will recognize the signs if we pay attention. But these signs foretell of the end for mankind collectively. The end of our lives individually is also something only God knows and determines.

Who God is during this transition from this era into the realm of eternity is a role only He can fill. God will be our Judge. He is the only one who can carry out that responsibility perfectly. We will read exactly what happens on Judgment Day, but as for who God is on that Day, He tells us:

> "The Father judges no one. Instead, he has given the Son absolute authority to judge, so that everyone will honor the Son, just as they honor the Father." John 5:22-23 NLT

Suffice it to say for now that who we believe God to be in this lifetime will determine our eternal destiny, it will determine the final verdict He will pronounce. We will be there to see that life will ultimately be fair, based upon our choice.

God tells us that our verdict will determine which of the two ultimate destinations will be ours – Heaven or Hell.

The next Chapter – *Who Am I?* will bring us to an understanding of ourselves from God's perspective.

Chapter 3

Who Am I?

We are all a part of a collective group of people known as the human race. Although that provides some sense of belonging, it falls short of a deeper-seeded search for our individual identity. Most of us have learned that there are no two people who are exactly alike, both physically and in character. We are unique, one-of-a-kind individuals. While that, too, helps us to answer the question "Who am I?" it does not give us the answer we are looking for.

The quest for the answer to this question is rooted in the fact that we all want to know we are here for a reason, a higher purpose that will eventually lead to something better. This drive to know our purpose is spiritually driven. We are more than a creature that appears for a few years, then fades into a vapor of a memory to a small group of people. After a couple of generations, few, if any, ever knew we existed.

If someone were to ask us: "Who are you?" we would probably start out by telling them our name. If we go further to identify ourselves, we would mention the things that we relate to the most: family, friends, what we do for a living, etc. However, these are simply the garnish of our identity. Who we are has everything to do with our character, our inner being, our spirit. Our character only shows itself in relationships over time, in different situations. It stands to reason that only the people we spend time with know who we really are. Interestingly enough, we discover things about ourselves we never knew as we go through life experiences for the first time.

The good news is we are more than what we can ever imagine, because we were created on purpose in the very image of God Himself. He made us with a specific purpose in mind. God has plans for each one of us that, if we follow His leading, will not only have an impact here on this planet at this time, but will impact us and others for all of eternity.

God did not make these plans for us without regard to others. One of the most fascinating aspects of each individual plan is the beauty of how God designed them to mesh with others without us losing our individual identity. All of these individual plans converge with God's master plan for humanity. This blending together of individual plans is designed to bring out the best in us as individuals, as well as everyone else. The substance of these plans is founded in relationships. These relationships started at the very beginning of time and will continue until the end arrives.

To fully understand the answer to the question of "Who am I?" we have to go back to the very beginning. This will help us realize how we got here, why we are where we are, and discover where we are going both individually and collectively.

Our Heritage – In The Beginning

All of us have a beginning. That beginning is a result of the decision made by others – first by God, then by our father and mother. Where we come from has an incredible effect on who we are and who we can become. The beginning for all of us starts with the very first human beings – Adam and Eve.

After God created the Heavens and the Earth, He created the first man - Adam.

> "The Lord God formed the man from the dust of the ground and breathed into his nostrils the breath of life, and the man became a living being." Genesis 2:7 NIV

God created and infused into Adam a spirit by breathing into him the breath of life. This is what makes us unlike any other animal. Our spirits are the substance of our being and identity. The truly amazing thing about our spirit is that it is made in God's image. It has the incredible capability of being a reflection of our creator. God tells us plainly:

"So God created man in his own image, in the image of God he created him," Genesis 1:27 NIV

Adam was made in God's image meaning, that he reflected God's character. We have a saying that captures this similarity on the human side: "Like father, like son." When God created Adam, he made him perfect in every way, physically and spiritually. When God created Adam, He brought him to life out of non-existence and into an existence that would go on for all eternity. Just as we are created in God's image, once created we all become eternal beings. In the beginning, not only was Adam eternal from a spiritual standpoint, his body was designed to live for all eternity as well. His body was designed in a way that would allow him to fulfill God's plan for his life. This instinctive knowledge is further confirmed as God tells us:

"... He has also set eternity in the hearts of men..." Ecclesiastes 3:11 NIV

After God completed His creative work, He reflected on what He had done, not only with Adam but with His entire creation:

"God saw all that he had made, and it was very good." Genesis 1:31 NIV

He saw the beauty and full potential of everything He had created. Everything was perfect and working together just the way He designed and intended. Once God finished creating, He began to interact with His creation, especially with mankind. His interaction with Adam expressed itself in the development of a relationship.

God knew Adam completely and Adam was just getting to know God. As with the development of any relationship, it requires the investing of time with each other. The relationship between God, Adam and Eve was unlike anything we can ever experience now, as God actually lived with Adam:

> *"... the LORD God as he was walking in the garden in the cool of the day..." Gen 3:8 NIV*

Life was not confined to just communing with each other. God wanted to share the caring for and cultivating of His creation. God put into motion the plans He had for Adam. God was actually entering into a partnership with Adam by turning the caring for this planet over to Adam, starting him out first in the Garden of Eden:

> *"The Lord God took the man and put him in the Garden of Eden to work it and take care of it." Genesis 2:15 NIV*

Adam took his position of authority as God intended. His first task was to subdue the animals and name them, which he did faithfully. After a while, it became apparent to Adam that he needed more companionship than what the animals could provide. God knew this as well:

> *"The Lord God said, "It is not good for the man to be alone. I will make a helper suitable for him"... So the Lord God caused the man to fall into a deep sleep; and while he was sleeping, he took one of the man's ribs and closed up the place with flesh. Then the Lord God made a woman from the rib he had taken out of the man, and he brought her to the man." Gen 2:18-22 NIV*

Adam was now entering into another relationship and shared in his responsibilities with her. They enjoyed each other's company. Day by day, they grew in knowledge, understanding, wisdom and character. They reached the "age" of accountability, with God holding them responsible for their decisions. God gave Adam and

Eve everything they needed. Along with this partnering came great liberties, benefits, responsibilities and choices:

> *"You are free to eat from any tree in the garden; but you must not eat from the tree of the knowledge of good and evil, for when you eat of it you will surely die." Genesis 2:16-17 NIV*

As any good father would do, God instructed and warned Adam about the consequences of a poor choice – that of eating from the forbidden tree. God made clear to Adam the consequence of ignoring His warning. The death God was talking about was not only a physical one, but a spiritual one as well. But God created mankind to be free will beings – that is, He gave us the ability to choose for ourselves, even if those choices were harmful, and how they would negatively affect others. What happened next changed everything for themselves and everyone else:

> *"She took some and ate it. She also gave some to her husband, who was with her, and he ate it." Genesis 3:6 NIV*

Adam and Eve were now going to live with the consequences of their choice. As a result of their choice, God, who is the same yesterday, today and forever, had to separate Himself from them:

> *"So the Lord God banished [Adam] from the Garden of Eden ... he drove the man out," Genesis 3:23-24 NIV*

The relationship between man and God had been broken because of Adam's and Eve's choice. God, perfect in every way, could no longer be with man, who as a result of his choice, was no longer perfect. The first part of the death consequence God warned Adam about took hold in the form of a spiritual death – separation from God. It would later result in physical death - their bodies were now destined to die.

We are all descendants from Adam and Eve and as such, all of their descendents would inherit their spiritual and physical conditions. We inherited the spiritual separation from God; our bodies became temporary shells that contain our spirits. God tells us:

"One man sinned, and so death ruled all people because of that one man." Romans 5:17 NCV

This very brief history explains why we needed to go back to the beginning to understand why we too are not in the relationship with God that He intended. It also explains why our planet is deteriorating, as man continues to make poor, selfish choices.

If that were the end of the story, we would be right in despairing – there would be no hope for us. As we read in the last chapter, God did give us hope – hope that would become a reality for us only if we believe what God did for us.

Individually – The Here and Now

Now that we have a better understanding of who we are from our heritage standpoint, we now need to focus on who we are as individuals. Just as God created Adam and Eve, He created each one of us in His image with eternal purpose. In spite of all our failings and shortcomings, we are nothing less than amazing. Here are the words God uses to describe how marvelous a work we are as individuals:

".. amazingly and miraculously made." Psalm 139:14 God's Word

"For you created my inmost being; you knit me together in my mother's womb ... I am fearfully and wonderfully made; your works are wonderful ... my frame was not hidden from you when I was made in the secret place. When I was woven together in the depths of the earth, your eyes saw my unformed body. All the days ordained for me were written in your book before one of them came to be." Psalm 139:13-16 NIV

We are all precious and special in His sight, so much so that He determined the time and place we were to live in history:

"[God] determined the times set for [us] and the exact places where [we] should live." Acts 17:26 NIV

We are not here by chance or accident. God had you in mind from the very beginning – no one is a mistake no matter how we got here. We are here by His choosing and design. So why did God pick this time and this place for us? That became even more important in light of the fact we are all born separated from God, and His desire is for each one of us to choose to bridge that gap:

"God did this so that men would seek him and perhaps reach out for him and find him, though he is not far from each one of us." Acts 17:27 NIV

This is our time and place in history because God wanted each one of us to have the best opportunity to grow in our knowledge, wisdom and character in order to have a personal relationship with Him. We were deliberately placed where we are:

"you have come ...for such a time as this" Ester 4:14 NIV

Just as God had a special plan and purpose for Adam and Eve, He has a specific, tailored plan just for you as well. These plans are not just to get you through day-by-day, but to get you to your intended eternal position through the development of your spiritual character. We shortchange God and ourselves by settling for the short-term "gain," which is usually not much more than trying to please ourselves. Our impatience causes us to be very near-sighted. If we deliberately follow God's plans, there will be long-term rewards beyond anything we could ever imagine. God tells us the intent and benefits of His plan in helping us know who we are in His sight:

"I know what I'm doing. I have it all planned out — plans to take care of you, not abandon you, plans to give you the future you hope for." Jeremiah 29:11 The Message

We are much more than flesh and blood. When Adam and Eve separated themselves from God, they doomed their bodies to die. We know very well that our bodies will also die, one day returning to dust. Not that we need a lot of reminding, but God confirms what we already know:

"everyone must die once" Hebrews 9:27 NCV

And ...

"[we] came from dust and [we] return to dust" Ecclesiastes 3:20 NLT

It is amazing, though, how we spend so much more time on the part of us that will die than on the spiritual matters that will affect us for all eternity. Many people spend incredible amounts of time and energy to get into shape and stay healthy. It is definitely something we should do – take care of ourselves, but we should be careful to do at least the same for our spirits. We also form most of our opinions of others, at least initially, by their external appearances. God pays no attention to what we place such high value on:

"The Lord does not look at the things man looks at. Man looks at the outward appearance, but the Lord looks at the heart." 1 Samuel 16:7 NIV

God is making it crystal clear here that getting into Heaven is simply and exclusively a matter of the heart. Since our primary interest here is getting into Heaven, we will no longer address who we are in terms of our physical appearance.

What is imperative for us to come to terms with individually is the fact that when we are born into this world, we are dead spiritually to God – every one of us. Unless we change who we are from that perspective, we are condemned to stay that way for all eternity.

We read in the last chapter what God has already done to make the only way for us to change the course of our eternal destiny. God did not just pull away after making this way for us to get back into relationship with Him; He is constantly pointing the way through the circumstances and people in our lives. How we respond to these God-given opportunities will determine if we stay separated from God or bridge that gap forever.

The key to making this eternal change is once again a matter of the heart. Only when we become spiritually childlike will we see our true state of being separated from God, our need for Him, and our hopelessness without Him. It is when we try to apply brain power to a spiritual matter that hinders us the most:

"[God] has hidden these things from the wise and learned, and revealed them to little children." Matthew 11:25 NIV

God gets to the core of what we must do to eliminate this barrier. We must reflect the character of a child before we can ever have a relationship with God.

"I tell you the truth, unless you change and become like little children, you will never enter the kingdom of heaven." Matthew 18:3-4 NIV

What Jesus meant when He said *"become like little children,"* has everything to do with our heart's disposition. We educate ourselves to the point where we think we are wise and sophisticated, instead of realizing we are becoming more callous and prideful. Not even the people closest to us really know who we are because of the walls we set up. As a result, most adults have a very difficult time reverting to this childlike disposition God requires, because it makes us vulnerable and we even risk looking foolish in the eyes of others.

The matters of the heart are defined by our choices. We are known by what we do. The moral choices we make can be categorized as either being right or wrong. This judgment is primarily made by what man defines within each culture. Most importantly, what God judges will make an eternity of difference. What is God's standard and how are we supposed to know what that is? God equipped each one of us with the knowledge of right and wrong:

"I will put my laws in their hearts, and I will write them on their minds." Hebrews 10:16 NIV

It is for this very reason that we have a conscience that tells us what is right and what is wrong. It is not so that we will feel bad, He wants us to come to terms with our spiritual condition:

"... through the law we become conscious of sin." Romans 3:20 NIV

As a result of sin, we are separated from God, and therefore we fall short of who we need to be to have a personal relationship with God:

"All have sinned and are not good enough for God's glory." Romans 3:23 NCV

We need God to get us from who we are on our own, to who we can be with His help. God promises if we look for what He has already done, we can become the person He planned for us to be. God promised:

"Ask and it will be given to you; seek and you will find; knock and the door will be opened to you." Matthew 7:7 NIV

So what is it we should be looking for, and how will we know when we find it? You have already started your search when you picked up this book. This is more than a search from simple curiosity, it is a search motivated from your heart. It's a search that is very much like one a little child would make - earnestly seeking to know something. Then and only then will we find the answer.

Without this childlike heart, the search will seem foolish. We must trust and believe as a little child would when God speaks to us:

> *"Today, if you hear [My] voice, do not harden your hearts."* Hebrews 3:7-8 NIV

How you respond to God will either move you closer to God or your heart will be hardened, pushing you further away from Him. The former response will bring you to a heartfelt desire to make things right between you and God; the latter will keep you away from God for all eternity. The key to which way you respond has everything to do with whether or not you believe, trust or have faith in God:

> *"And without faith it is impossible to please God, because anyone who comes to him must believe that he exists and that he rewards those who earnestly seek him."* Hebrews 11:6 NIV

When it comes to our eternal destiny, God is allowing us to make our own decision. No one is bound by Adam's and Eve's decision. As we read in the last chapter, God made a way for each one of us to make our own decision regarding our eternal destiny – hence, who we become based upon our decision. God has made His desire known to us – He wants every person to spend eternity with Him. God made His decision and a way; now we need to make ours.

Since our decision is one of eternal consequence, we need to be aware that there are others who are also interested in what choice we make. These are mainly people who want us to be with them after life on this side of eternity ends. Do not be naïve enough, however, to think that there aren't others who are trying to keep you from knowing the truth. These individuals understand what is at stake and are doing everything they can to prevent you from being who you were intended to be:

> *"The devil who rules this world has blinded the minds of those who do not believe. They cannot see the light of the*

Good News — the Good News about the glory of Christ, who is exactly like God." 2 Corinthians 4:4 NCV

The devil and his cohorts will try to lead you to an ever-increasing distain for God and all that He represents. Just as God warned Adam of the consequence of making a choice that would separate him from God, God warns us today of that same consequence, only this time there will be no second chances. This is the warning for today for those who ignore God's promptings to turn to Him:

"They are darkened in their understanding and separated from the life of God because of the ignorance that is in them due to the hardening of their hearts." Ephesians 4:18 NIV

Little children understand things better when they are simple. In order for us to become children of God, we must make our choice to become childlike in our hearts. God made the entire process of becoming who He intended us to become so simple that many are very skeptical. The reaction becomes one where we hear: "That's too good to be true." This skepticism is well founded, since most "offers" we receive are from men who have ulterior motives. God only has us in mind – what could possibly be more like God than to make this a simple transaction of the heart, where we acknowledge and accept what He tells us?

He wants us to take our intended position in the family of God. He wants you to trust Him with your eternal destiny by becoming the person He knows you can be. Exactly how you accept this gift He is offering unfolds as you continue to read through this book.

Our time on Earth is limited. We did not pick the time when we entered, and God has determined the day when we depart. We must choose while there still is time.

Destiny – The Eternal

We are eternal beings that can only go on to one of two ultimate destinations after our bodies die and our life here comes to an end. As eternal beings, we continue to live. Where we go is something man has debated for centuries. Some believe we come back to life here on Earth in some form and get another chance. Others believe we just cease to exist. The majority of people believe we will either go to Heaven or Hell. This last group is in line with what God tells us. Many people and religions have a concept of what it takes to get into Heaven, but they don't have it right. Remember, religions are manmade institutions, and therefore prone to error. Individuals as well may have their own set of beliefs, based on what makes sense them. But the only thing that really matters is what God says.

People have come up with ways and sometimes elaborate systems that are logical in how we can get to Heaven. These ways have everything to do with our behavior as we live our lives day by day. Most of them are performance-based, with a hope that they have figured out the threshold of performance that will qualify them to get into Heaven.

Every one of these approaches fails to recognize that Heaven is a place of perfection and only those who are perfect in the sight of God will be allowed to enter in. Yes, who you are, based upon your heart condition as it relates to God, is all that matters. There is nothing we can do through our own efforts in our lifetime that gets us to a state of perfection required to get into Heaven. God did for us what we cannot do for ourselves – who we are in our hearts will determine where we end up. God may be all-powerful, but He has given us the power to stay separated from Him.

We will discover who we are by how we respond to God. God's way to heaven is our choice. If we reject His way for whatever reason, we will never enter into Heaven and remain on the course we are born into – the path to Hell and eternal separation from God. Be careful that you are not rejecting God's way simply because you think you are rejecting someone's opinion or religion. Who we choose to become in light of all eternity is explained in the chapters that follow.

Chapter 4

Selection Criteria

Are there specific criteria God uses to determine who gets into Heaven, or do we just try to do the "right things" and hope for the best? What do I have to do to pass God's test? If there are criteria that apply to our lives that determine if we go to Heaven, what are they? These are not only valid questions, the answers are critical to anyone who wants to get into Heaven. God is the one who put these standards in place and ingrained them into our very being – everyone without exception - because God makes sure we have everything it takes to make the choice of where we spend eternity.

Man's Criteria

When it comes to setting up a standard for what it takes to get to Heaven, we soon see that man's criteria are based on how well we perform. Let's look more closely at how that plays out in the lives of many. For those who think about wanting to go to Heaven, we do think about what we have to do to make sure we get there. We set up criteria in our minds as to what we think it takes to get into Heaven.

Since God has given everyone the innate knowledge of right and wrong, we know instinctively when we are violating God's principles, and we feel guilty. We know that we don't always make the right choices, but for the most part we reason that we live a pretty good life – obviously nothing that would merit being sent to Hell. There are individuals, however, that most would agree would be sent to Hell by God because of their wickedness or evil deeds – take Hitler or Edi Amine as two in more recent history. When people set up their own criteria, they are usually pretty subjective in nature, giving us no clear-cut line to indicate when good is just not good enough to get you into Heaven. As we will soon see, God makes it crystal clear with no room for doubt.

What are some of the ways we apply criteria in our everyday lives? One is how people apply established criteria to determine the results of tests. The example most of us can relate to where criteria are used is in school. We go to classes, study and take tests. The test results show if we have reached a certain level of proficiency to move on to the next grade. The subjective part of these criteria shows up when, many times, teachers find themselves grading on a curve so more students are given a passing grade, based on how well the student does compared to the other students. Another example is when we apply for a job, there are qualifications (criteria) the employer sets for the position. We go in for the interview and wonder how well we did. Our next thought is about how well we did compared to the other candidates, to figure out if we have a good chance of being selected.

So then when it comes to the criteria many think are reasonable in what it takes to get into Heaven, we start to compare ourselves to others as a way of thinking we are OK. Because this sounds so logical and reasonable, millions buy into it. We figure we have to earn our way into Heaven by living "good" lives, thinking good thoughts, going to religious services every once in a while, and doing good deeds. We think we will have passed God's tests of life, and then God just has to let us in. After all, He is a loving God, and we reason, "I'm a pretty good person. Sure, I've made my mistakes, but who hasn't? Next to so-n-so, I'm not so bad."

Unfortunately, we tend to impose this type of reasoning to how God will determine who gets into Heaven. If we live our lives based on this approach, we will definitely not make it into Heaven. Anything or anyone who tells you to rely on this comparative approach on how you get to Heaven is absolutely contrary to what God tells us.

But to illustrate that getting into Heaven is not simply good deeds, God gives us the instruction we need in this following account:

"One day one of the local officials asked him, 'Good Teacher, what must I do to deserve eternal life?' Jesus said, 'Why are you calling me good? No one is good — only God. You know the commandments, don't you? No illicit sex, no killing, no stealing, no lying, honor your father and mother.' He said, 'I've kept them all for as long as I can remember.' When Jesus heard that, he said, 'Then there's only one thing left to do: Sell everything you own and give it away to the poor. You will have riches in heaven. Then come, follow me.' This was the last thing the official expected to hear. He was very rich and became terribly sad. He was holding on tight to a lot of things and not about to let them go. Seeing his reaction, Jesus said, 'Do you have any idea how difficult it is for people who have it all to enter God's kingdom? I'd say it's easier to thread a camel through a needle's eye than get a rich person into God's kingdom.' 'Then who has any chance at all?' the others asked. 'No chance at all,' Jesus said, 'if you think you can pull it off by yourself, every chance in the world if you trust God to do it.'" Luke 18:18-27 The Message

Then there is the approach that the way to get to Heaven is dependent on how well we abide by rules and regulations that God has put in place. This is a performance-based approach with defined criteria, and is still devoid of the relational part of life with God. The most prominent manmade institutions that follow this approach are religions.

Religions usually start with very noble purposes with the ultimate objective of drawing closer to God as best they know how. Some do a better job of doing this than others. The tendency, though, is that the rules, regulations and ceremonies they set up turn into stale step-by-step formulas and miss the relational part of what God requires. This is the reverse of what we will see God requires in order for us to get into Heaven. Once you have a relationship, then and only then does what you do serve as evidence of the reality of the relationship.

The danger comes when following rules and regulations becomes the dominant theme. Compounding this problem is when the leaders within the religion teach that the following of the rules and regulations is all that matters. The worst of all situations is when these religious individuals teach that approach with selfish motives. We often refer to these people as having a "holier than you" attitude – none of us like or are drawn to such individuals. This is when religion and its leaders become an obstacle rather than a help. Here is how God views it when that happens:

> *"Woe to you, teachers of the law and Pharisees, you hypocrites! You travel over land and sea to win a single convert, and when he becomes one, you make him twice as much a son of hell as you are." Matt 23:15 NIV*

Another example God gives us to illustrate this point of just being religious not being what God will use as His criteria — and this really needs to be emphasized — is in this account:

> *"Not everyone who says to me, 'Lord, Lord,' will enter the kingdom of heaven, but only he who does the will of my Father who is in heaven. Many will say to me on that day, 'Lord, Lord, did we not prophesy in your name, and in your name drive out demons and perform many miracles?' Then I will tell them plainly, 'I never knew you. Away from me, you evildoers!'" Matt 7:21-23 NIV*

And finally, one more account that drives the point home where the attitude of a religious leader is compared with an individual that society shunned:

> *"[Jesus] told his next story to some who were complacently pleased with themselves over their moral performance and looked down their noses at the common people: "Two men went up to the [church] to pray, one a [church leader], the*

other a tax man. The [church leader] posed and prayed like this: 'Oh, God, I thank you that I am not like other people — robbers, crooks, adulterers, or, heaven forbid, like this tax man. I fast twice a week and tithe on all my income.' Meanwhile the tax man, slumped in the shadows, his face in his hands, not daring to look up, said, 'God, give mercy. Forgive me, a sinner.'" Jesus commented, "This tax man, not the other, went home made right with God. If you walk around with your nose in the air, you're going to end up flat on your face, but if you're content to be simply yourself, you will become more than yourself." Luke 18:9-14 NIV

Now we know what doesn't work and what trips up most people. Now let's see what God tells us are His criteria.

God's Criteria

In dramatic contrast to man's way of thinking of what it takes to get into Heaven, God tells us that we only have to do one thing. That's right, God only has one criterion that you either meet or you will never enter into His Kingdom in Heaven!

So what is this one thing we all have to do to get into Heaven? God tells us that it's having a personal relationship with Him. You may be asking: "OK, so just how do I do that? How can I have a relationship with God, who is holy and perfect in every way" You might think that it's impossible to have a personal relationship with God, but He tells us otherwise:

"Jesus looked at them and said, 'With man this is impossible, but with God all things are possible.'" Matt 19:26 NIV

The impossible was overcome when Jesus came down from Heaven to bridge that impossible gap between Him and us – perfection to imperfection. He came and walked among us because He loves us beyond what we can understand, and demonstrated that love. This is the sacrifice God made:

"This is how much God loved the world: He gave his Son, his one and only Son. And this is why: so that no one need be destroyed; by believing in him, anyone can have a whole and lasting life. God didn't go to all the trouble of sending his Son merely to point an accusing finger, telling the world how bad it was. He came to help, to put the world right again. Anyone who trusts in him is acquitted." John 3:16-18 The Message

God knew exactly what it would take to make a way for us to have a personal relationship with Him. He had to die in our place, paying the price for our sins, thereby bridging the gap to make a way for us to have a personal relationship with Him. When He did this, He paid the full price of admission into Heaven for those who ask to have a relationship with Him. What Jesus did is recorded in this and many other accounts by eyewitnesses:

"... Christ died for our sins according to the Scriptures, that he was buried, that he was raised on the third day according to the Scriptures." 1 Corinthians 15:3-4 NIV

Not only did He die in our place, but to demonstrate that death no longer could have its hold on us, God raised Him from the dead. This also shows us that God can raise us from the dead to make good His promise of spending eternity with Him in Heaven when we accept His gift of salvation:

"Jesus and has given us a position in heaven with him. He did this through Christ Jesus out of his generosity to us in order to show his extremely rich kindness in the world to come. God [saves] you through faith as an act of kindness. You [have] nothing to do with it. Being saved is a gift from God. It's not the result of anything you've done, so no one can brag about it." Ephesians 2:6-10 NIV

As with anything that seems too good to be true, even when God is in the middle, we tend to think we are the exception to the rule.

Some of you may be thinking: "There is no way God would ever want a personal relationship with me, because I've done some really bad things in my life!" Or, you may be thinking that you have to clean up your life, give things up, or make changes before you could ever approach God. None of that will pave the way to a relationship with God, because He accepts you just the way you are.

So just how do we approach God to have this relationship? First and foremost, God tells us we must approach Him as a little child would come to a loving parent: attentive, responsive, submissive, innocent, humble, vulnerable, open, trusting and seeking. Arrogance and pride are just the opposite attitudes and will do nothing but widen the gap between you and God. God makes this clear in what He tells us here:

> *"Let the little children come to me, and do not hinder them, for the kingdom of God belongs to such as these. I tell you the truth, anyone who will not receive the kingdom of God like a little child will never enter it." Mark 10:14-16 NIV*

It's our demeanor that initiates what it takes to have this personal relationship with God. Children have basic needs in their lives, and they know where to go to have those needs met. When we have the demeanor of a child, we recognize just how much we need God in our lives. And once we approach God as a child, He responds. Here is what God says we need to do to begin a relationship with Him:

> *"'The word is near you; it is in your mouth and in your heart,' that is, the word of faith we are proclaiming: That if you confess with your mouth, 'Jesus is Lord,' and believe in your heart that God raised him from the dead, you will be saved." Romans 10:8-9 NIV*

When we say this with all sincerity of heart, we are acknowledging what God did for us, and recognize that we cannot do what only God can do – make a way for imperfect beings to be made whole again, making our peace with Him. Here is another way God puts it so we can better understand:

"God has set everything right between him and me!" Scripture reassures us, "No one who trusts God like this — heart and soul — will ever regret it." It's exactly the same no matter what a person's religious background may be: the same God for all of us, acting the same incredibly generous way to everyone who calls out for help. "Everyone who calls, 'Help, God!' gets help." Romans 10:9-13 The Message

God is reemphasizing that this is strictly a matter of the heart on our part, and us accepting His free gift of eternal life. Here is another account that brings that point home:

"For it is by grace you have been saved, through faith — and this not from yourselves, it is the gift of God" Ephesians 2:8 NIV

The only "ingredient" we add to the passing of the gift of everlasting life with God is faith – or more simply put – believing what God is telling us here is true and we trust Him implicitly. We put our faith or trust in many things each day. From the simplest things like when we sit in a chair, we trust it will hold us; to the more complex, when we have faith in the doctor who is operating on our hearts. So we must have the faith to place our trust in what God tells us.

What About The Ten Commandments?

By now you may be thinking: "Well what about the Ten Commandments? Don't they have anything to do with getting into Heaven?" Almost everyone has heard of the Ten Commandments, even if you are not a part of the Christian/Judeo community. There is even a classic movie that was made by the same name that is broadcast every year on many television stations around the world. One of the most dramatic scenes is when Moses goes up Mount Sinai and God carves out the Ten Commandments on stone tablets.

In case you don't know them, or maybe have forgotten some of them, here they are in a summarized version capturing the intent from a relationship standpoint:

God spoke all these words:

1. "You will have no other gods, only Me.
2. Don't create your own gods.
3. Don't use my name in curses or put up with the irreverent use of My name.
4. Set aside one day a week to rest, using that time to develop your relationship with Me and others.
5. Honor your father and mother so that you'll live a long time.
6. Do not murder.
7. Do not commit adultery.
8. Do not steal.
9. Do not lie about your neighbor.
10. Do not lust after your neighbor's possessions or wife. Don't set your heart on anything that is your neighbor's." Exodus 20:1-17 NIV

Just how do these commandments fit in with getting into Heaven? Since God only has one criterion to get anyone into Heaven, the Ten Commandments don't have anything to do with it. But they do serve an extremely important purpose. God gave us these commandments not to save us, but to show us that we are imperfect sinners and therefore separated from God. More importantly, it drives home the point that we need God to rescue us from our current destiny. This is how God puts it:

"We know that the law's commands are for those who have the law. This stops all excuses and brings the whole world under God's judgment because no one can be made right with God by following the law. The law only shows us our sin." Romans 3:19-20 NCV

As was mentioned before, God only has one criterion to get into Heaven – having a personal relationship with Him, and if we examine more closely the first Commandment, that is the one that establishes the fact we must have a relationship with Him before any of the other Commandments play into our lives. And what does that mean? Quite simply, it means that IF we have a personal relationship with God, we will prove it by how we live our lives, motivated to love God by not violating any of the other Commandments. But as we read earlier in the chapter, just being disciplined enough to abide by "the rules" does not prove you have a relationship with God. What we do in life, motivated by our love for God, will be all the evidence needed to prove to ourselves that our relationship with Him is real.

Many people have difficulty remembering all Ten Commandments, so to make it even simpler for us, Jesus summarized these ten down to two:

> *"'Love the Lord your God with all your heart and with all your soul and with all your mind.' This is the first and greatest commandment. And the second is like it: 'Love your neighbor as yourself.' All the [Commandments] hang on these two commandments." Matthew 22:37-40 NIV*

Reflecting back on the Ten Commandments, we can see that the first four Commandments deal with our relationship with God. The other six Commandments are wrapped in loving your neighbor. We have a similar saying: Treat others as you would want them to treat you.

What most people get confused about is that God tells us that what we do proves what the motives of our hearts are all about. It is only AFTER we establish our relationship with Him that what we do counts for anything eternal. So when we do things with the right motives - love of God and the desire to share that love with others – it is the evidence and proof that we are in a relationship with God.

God's love is greater than any offense you may have committed. Remember, God knew everything you were going to do during your lifetime before He created you, so what you do never surprises God, and nothing you could ever do can block the way to forgiveness with Him when you are sincerely repentant. Otherwise we could legitimately say: "Why did God create me, knowing what I was going to do, and then make it impossible for me to change my heart?" Listen:

> *"What then shall we say? Is God unjust? Not at all! For he says...'I will have mercy on whom I have mercy, and I will have compassion on whom I have compassion.' It does not, therefore, depend on man's desire or effort, but on God's mercy." Rom 9:14-17 NIV*

And when God has mercy on us, miracles happen:

> *"Mercy triumphs over judgment!" James 2:13 NIV*

Don't believe that there is something you could ever have done that trumps God's love and thereby block your way into Heaven. That is a lie from the Devil, a voice from the pit of Hell. God tells us:

> *"The devil who rules this world has blinded the minds of those who do not believe. They cannot see the light of the Good News — the Good News about the glory of Christ, who is exactly like God." 2 Corinthians 4:4 NCV*

To summarize, God's criteria is a simple Pass-Fail one. He does not grade on a curve, nor does He judge us relative to how others lived their lives. The only thing that matters is our relationship with God and the evidence of it being genuine. The evidence is recorded in the Books God is keeping of choices we make and what we do with the right motives during our lifetime, that proves our relationship with Him is genuine. Judgment Day is when all of the real motives are revealed.

Chapter 5

Judgment Day

Judgment Day, the Last Judgment, the Day of Reckoning, the Day of the Lord, the Great Day - different names for the same thing. What comes to your mind when you hear one of these terms? Most people seem to know instinctively that such a day is really coming - that it is unavoidable. The most chilling part of it is the sense of its finality. Yet most people know very little, if anything, about what that fateful Day is all about, and what, if anything, they should be doing now in light of its eternal consequences.

    Let's take this closer to home. What do you know about Judgment Day? You may be admitting "Not a lot." Then you ask yourself, "Who really knows for sure?" Many have tried to share what their take is on the subject. Hollywood has produced movies, and songs have been written about Judgment Day, based primarily on what they envision it to be. Hollywood's movie versions of Judgment Day usually deal with one person getting even with a "villain" who wronged him or her in some extreme capacity. They may make interesting action movies and stir up a lot of emotions, but they fail miserably at addressing the Day God set aside to make everything right. As for the songs, there are numerous ones that recognize the reality of Judgment Day, yet seem to have an "in your face" attitude where they are willing to wait to see what will happen to them on that Day.

Yet ignorance on anyone's part is not going to change anything that will happen to him or her on Judgment Day. If we are seriously interested in knowing the truth, we need to listen to the One who planned, designed, and set everything in motion regarding this Day. That One is none other than God Himself. Because He loves and cares so deeply for all of us, He actually shared with us what Judgment Day is, its purpose, and what will happen on that fateful day. Once you have been enlightened on the subject, you can then make informed decisions regarding what in your life needs to change.

Since Judgment Day will have such a permanent impact on every one of us, knowing what will happen on that Day becomes rather urgent. So what exactly does God tell us about that Day, and how does it affect you and me personally? Some of the most immediate and pressing questions people have, include:

- What is Judgment Day?
- What is the purpose of Judgment Day?
- What will happen on Judgment Day?

What Is Judgment Day?

As we get started, it first helps to begin by explaining what Judgment Day is not, which will dispel the misunderstandings many may have of this Day. Judgment Day is NOT a trial. If it were a trial, I believe God would have called it "Trial Day." You may be asking, "Well, just when is the trial?" Good question! Fortunately, the answer is quite simple. Your life on planet Earth is the "trial." If you are reading this, you still have the opportunity to affect the verdict. The "trial" is over for those who have already passed on. Their eternal destiny has already been determined.

So what is Judgment Day? Let's look at the parallel in our own court system. That parallel is when a judge pronounces the sentence; it's the time when the judge pronounces the verdict after deliberating the evidence. When an unwanted verdict has been pronounced, there is a faint hope of getting the verdict changed through the appeals process. However, on Judgment Day, there are no lawyers to argue your case, there are no loopholes, no appeals, or plea bargaining, or any other way to bypass the consequences of the choices we made during our lifetime. It will be totally irrelevant whether or not laws established by man allowed for such choices. All those laws did was postpone the inevitable consequences.

Judgment Day is what happens right after God ends the current era, before beginning the next one that will go on for all eternity. It is the Day God will pronounce each individual's eternal destiny, based upon the evidence of our lives as it is recorded in the Books and by testimonies given by eyewitnesses. Once all the verdicts have been pronounced, God will separate everyone into two groups. The first group includes those who will be spending all eternity with God, who will be on His right. The second group will be on His left, and will then be thrown in the Lake of Burning Sulfur for all eternity.

What Is The Purpose Of Judgment Day?

You may find yourself asking, "Why has God set a time when everyone will have to be judged, why not just let life go on as it is?" God is very patient, but He does have His limits. God gave mankind the opportunity to live in a perfect home in the beginning and take care of things on this planet, but we blew it. It doesn't take long after looking around to realize that since then, things are far from perfect and they aren't getting any better. We've proven time and again that we just can't get it right once and for all – on a human race level or on an individual basis.

Nevertheless, God did not abandon us, He gave us a hope by letting us know He will make everything perfectly right again. That is why God has set a time when He will put an end to life as we know it, and separate those who do not want to live with God and those who demonstrated their love for Him by the way they lived.

What Will Happen On Judgment Day?

Now that we understand what Judgment day is and its purpose, we need to get a picture in our minds of how this Day will unfold.

Judgment Day begins with the gathering of all who will be judged by God in one place – in front of Him. As was already said, He will then separate everyone into two groups – one on His right and one on His left. Those on His right are referred to as "sheep," and those on His left as "goats." Once that separation is complete, God will make His pronouncement of where these two groups will be spending eternity. The following paragraphs address the following, so you can better understand what Judgment Day will be like:

- Who will be the judge?
- Who will be judged?
- What will be judged?
- How will it be judged?
- What will be the verdict and what does it mean?

Who Will Be The Judge?

The judges we have presiding in our courts are appointed based upon their qualifications. They have to have the right training, education, and experience if they are to carry out their responsibilities in a manner that will ensure the law is interpreted, applied and upheld as it pertains to the cases over which he or she will be presiding. Since the judges in our judicial system are human, they are prone to make mistakes in judgment. However, our "system" allows for corrections and reversals in sentencing when new evidence comes to light, or facts relating to the case unfold that may have interfered with rendering the right verdict.

Our system may be good and well for here and now, but, when it comes to the Last Judgment, everything has to be perfect and for good reason, as it declares the destiny of an individual for all eternity. Since the verdict is permanent and can never be reversed, there is no room for any misunderstandings, lapses in judgment, or incomplete or flawed evidence. There is only one way to ensure perfection that Day – God Himself will have to be the prevailing judge. As we read in the Chapter *Who is God?*, we came to realize or affirm that He is perfect in every way – all-knowing, all-powerful. That makes Him totally qualified and able to carry out the judgment to perfection.

That includes knowing everyone's deepest motives for everything we have said, thought or done – something only God can do.

In the Chapter *Who is God?* we also read about God being one in three distinct persons Father, Son and Holy Spirit. All equal, all God. Again, this is something we cannot fully understand, but that revelation about God is particularly important as it relates to the Last Judgment. So, let's take the time to revisit what God tells us about Himself and the person of Jesus the Christ. Here is what God tells us:

> *"[Jesus], being in very nature God, did not consider* **equality** *with God something to be grasped ... being made in human likeness. And being found in appearance as a man, he humbled himself and became obedient to death — even death on a cross! Therefore God exalted him to the highest place and gave him the name that is above every name, that at* **the name of Jesus every knee should bow, in heaven and on earth and under the earth, and every tongue confess that Jesus Christ is [God]** *Philippians 2:6-11 NIV*

Jesus is not merely a good man or prophet who lived two thousand years ago, as so many contend –maybe even hope - He is none other than God almighty who took on our human nature. He took on human likeness and became a man Himself. He walked in our shoes, learned what it was like to be a human being, and experienced the challenges we face daily. This further qualified Him fully to be able to judge us in every way – perfectly. No one will be able to say, "You don't know what it was like, what I had to go through!" Because of Jesus' unique qualifications, God the Father appointed Him as the judge to preside on Judgment Day. Before now, you may not have heard of or realized Jesus' role as the presiding judge on this Day, but now that has been made clear. Here is what God tells us so that there are no doubts about that fact:

> *"God overlooked people's ignorance about these things in earlier times, but now he commands everyone everywhere to repent of their sins and turn to him. For he has set a day for*

judging the world with justice by the man he has appointed, and he proved to everyone who this is by raising him from the dead." Acts 17:30-31 NLT

He expounds on Jesus' role as judge:

"In addition, the Father judges no one. Instead, he has given the Son absolute authority to judge, so that everyone will honor the Son, just as they honor the Father. Anyone who does not honor the Son is certainly not honoring the Father who sent him." John 5:22-23 NLT

He clarifies and reinforces this by telling us:

"this will take place on the day when God will judge men's secrets through Jesus Christ" Romans 2:16 NIV

God makes it perfectly clear. The Judge is God himself in the person of Jesus, perfectly qualified to render perfect judgment. If you still reject in your mind and heart that Jesus is Himself God, God the Father warns us that we have in essence rejected Him. There is no greater rejection we can make in our lives! So, if you are "stuck" on this point - Jesus being God Himself — ask God to open your eyes to the truth, and He will do it.

Who Will Be Judged?

Considering this is the *last* Judgment, everyone who ever lived will have to be present on this Day. Even though this is the Day every human being will be judged, it is interesting and even significant to know that Satan and all of the fallen angels will also be judged on this Day. This all-encompassing Judgment Day further attests that there will not be any other day when judgment will be rendered. Here are the passages where God affirms who will be judged that Day:

*"For we must **all** stand before Christ to be judged. We will each receive whatever we deserve for the good or evil we have done in this earthly body." 2 Corinthians 5:10 NLT*

*"I saw **all** the dead, great and small, standing there—before the Throne!... Sea released its dead, Death and Hell turned in their dead. Each man and woman was judged by the way he or she had lived." Revelation 20:12-13 The Message*

"And the angels who did not keep their positions of authority but abandoned their own home these he has kept in darkness, bound with everlasting chains for judgment on the great Day." Jude 6 NIV

Once again, God makes it perfectly clear that all of mankind from all time will be there on that Day. That includes everyone from Adam and Eve to the last person who will ever be created. No one will be forgotten; no one will be left out. From the most famous and infamous people, to the most forsaken or forgotten individual who ever lived. People will be raised from the dead – regardless of when they lived, where they lived, their race, social status, or what religion they belonged to.

Another reason why everyone will be there is because God tells us that there just won't be anywhere else to be – there is no opting out of this happening:

*"Then I saw a great white throne and him who was seated on it. **Earth and sky fled from his presence, and there was no place for them.** Revelation 20:1 NIV*

It should be sobering, knowing beyond any doubt that we will be among the billions of others on that Day standing before Jesus, the subjects of God's judgment.

What Will Be Judged?

Try to imagine yourself there on Judgment Day with literally billions of others – We start to wonder as we stand there before Jesus, "What is He going to bring up about me? How is He going to judge what I did? What verdict will He pronounce?" Dare I say, with just these few questions, that it will be a time of great anxiety for everyone.

What we should realize at this point is that neither you nor I will have any control or influence on what and how we will be judged. This is shocking news to many who are used to relying on their own resources to ensure they get what they want. But since they won't be able to dig into their bank accounts, contact their lawyers or people who had power to make things "right," they will have no choice but to face the full brunt of the consequences of their decisions. Everything we have relied upon to get us out from under some predicament will not be there to rely upon at the Last Judgment.

> *"He will say: "Now where are their gods,... they took refuge in...? Let them rise up to help you! Let them give you shelter! See now that I myself am He! There is no god besides me. I put to death and bring to life, I have wounded and I will heal, and no one can deliver out of my hand. I lift my hand to heaven and declare: As surely as I live forever, when I sharpen my flashing sword and my hand grasps it in judgment, I will take vengeance on my adversaries and repay those who hate me." Deuteronomy 32:37-41 NIV*

This should send a shiver down our spine and give a heightened sense of urgency and concern to know precisely what and how we will be judged.

All during our lives, we all had the freedom to choose. Now, all of our choices will be measured by God, by His standards which have never changed, nor will they ever change. We are going to be held accountable for what we have done, are now doing, and will do before we die. There will be no justifying our actions or point to some law established by man that allowed our choice.

Going to the source, God tells us **what** He will be judging:

"Eventually God will bring everything that we do out into the open and judge it according to its hidden intent, whether it's good or evil." Ecclesiastes 12:14 NLT

"But I tell you that men will have to give account on the Day of Judgment for every careless word they have spoken." Matthew 12:36 NIV

"Nothing in all creation is hidden from God's sight. Everything is uncovered and laid bare before the eyes of him to whom we must give account." Hebrews 4:13 NIV

"The time is coming when everything that is covered up will be revealed, and all that is secret will be made known to all. Whatever you have said in the dark will be heard in the light, and what you have whispered behind closed doors will be shouted from the housetops for all to hear!" Luke 12:2-3 NLT

How Will We Be Judged?

Now that we come to the point where there can be no doubt about what God will be judging (everything), we need to understand just **how** will we be judged?

The first point we have to understand is that we are judged against God's standards. "Well," we may object, "I didn't know God's standards, so how can God judge me against something I didn't know anything about?" Sorry, that isn't even close to an acceptable excuse. Everyone intuitively knows right from wrong. That holds true no matter when or where they lived, what their social standing may have been, or what their religion may have taught. We **know** when we are making wrong choices. The reason we know God's standards intuitively is because that is how God designed us. God's "laws" are "written" on everyone's heart, so we are indeed without excuse. But don't take my word for it, read on:

They demonstrate that God's law is written in their hearts, for their own conscience and thoughts either accuse them or tell them they are doing right. And this is the message I proclaim—that the day is coming when God, through Christ Jesus, will judge everyone's secret life. Romans 2:15, 16 NLT

"If you sin without knowing what you're doing, God takes that into account. But if you sin knowing full well what you're doing, that's a different story entirely. Merely hearing God's law is a waste of your time if you don't do what he commands. Doing, not hearing, is what makes the difference with God.

When outsiders who have never heard of God's law follow it more or less by instinct, they confirm its truth by their obedience. They show that God's law is not something alien, imposed on us from without, but woven into the very fabric of our creation. There is something deep within them that echoes God's yes and no, right and wrong. Their response to God's yes and no will become public knowledge on the day God makes his final decision about every man and woman." Romans 2:12-16 The Message

The next point that we need to discuss is that God fully exposes a person's real motives. This is one way God guarantees a perfect verdict. Unlike the attributes and limitations of our judges, Jesus will have the full insight into the real motives of each person's actions. Nothing will be hidden from His sight that Day. God tells us that He knows peoples' motives:

"... He will bring to light what is hidden in darkness and will expose the motives of men's hearts." 1 Corinthians 4:5 NIV

"This will take place on the day when God will judge men's secrets through Jesus Christ" Romans 2:16 NIV

"... his eyes were like blazing fire." Revelation 1:14 NIV

The next part of how God will judge us may shock you. It is how God will make restitution and repay for every wrong committed. We have strong feelings when we see, or are the ones who have suffered, grave wrongs. We want the ones who inflicted the pain to "get what's coming to them" – in full measure.

God tells us to not get back at the ones who violated us. That's His job and He will definitely settle things up. Our desire is to try to make things right that are wrong - to right an injustice. But we must ultimately wait for God to render the perfect justice, completely and fully at the end of the world. What we have a hard time with is the timing of when God metes out that judgment. We need to be patient and leave that to God, because when He addresses the situation, nothing will be left undone. God says:

"Dear friends, never take revenge. Leave that to the righteous anger of God. For the Scriptures say, "I will take revenge; I will pay them back," says the Lord." Romans 12:19 NLT

We all have the desire for justice. It is something that is deep seeded within our being. All too often, we do not see justice meted out in our own judicial system. In fact, too often we see justice falling short due to some procedural breach, incomplete/faulty information, misrepresentations, fancy arguments that cloud the facts, or some other factor that short-circuits true justice. In short, our system is undeniably imperfect and life as we know it can be very unfair.

God is also interested in justice. He is the one in total control, and the only one who can right the wrongs of the ages. At the end of time, on Judgment Day, God has the last word; and until then, life remains unfair.

"For you will be treated as you treat others. The standard you use in judging is the standard by which you will be judged." Matthew 7:2 NLT

"Do not judge, and you will not be judged. Do not condemn, and you will not be condemned. Forgive, and you will be forgiven." Luke 6:37 NIV

Now let's remember here that we all deserve the full consequences of our choices. It's not just about the other guy getting his due; it's also about us getting ours as well. Yet there is a major difference between the two groups of people. Those who rejected Jesus and what He did to save them from the full consequences of their choices will get the full wrath of judgment. The others who acknowledged in their hearts what Jesus did for them on the cross will escape being separated from God for all eternity. Both sides of what happens on Judgment Day are addressed in this passage:

"There will be no mercy for those who have not shown mercy to others. But if you have been merciful, God will be merciful when he judges you." James 2:13 NLT

Putting it simply and to the point, those of us who reject Jesus as God and what He did for us will not be shown mercy and judged accordingly. Those who humbly realize they need to be rescued or saved from judgment, making their peace with God through Jesus the Christ, will be shown mercy and not condemned.

The following account dramatically sets the scene of how Judgment Day will unfold with the opening of The Books. This is last thing that happens before judgment begins:

"thrones were set in place, and the Ancient of Days [Jesus] took his seat. His clothing was as white as snow; the hair of his head was white like wool. His throne was flaming with fire, and its wheels were all ablaze. A river of fire was flowing, coming out from before him. Thousands upon thousands attended him; ten thousand times ten thousand stood before him. The court was seated, and the books were opened." Daniel 7:9-10 NIV

"And I saw the dead, great and small, standing before the throne, and books were opened." Revelation 20:12 NIV

This identifies the judge, the authority, the place and the vast crowds that will be there. Even though what is written in The Books would be proof enough of the perfect judgment, they are not the singular point of reference. As further evidence, there will also be witnesses who will step forward. God lets us know this in the following account:

"The men of Nineveh will stand up at the judgment with this generation and condemn it; for they repented at the preaching of Jonah, and now one greater than Jonah is here. The Queen of the South will rise at the judgment with this generation and condemn it; for she came from the ends of the earth to listen to Solomon's wisdom, and now one greater than Solomon is here." Matthew 12:41-42 NIV

And again:

"Yet it isn't I who will accuse you before the Father. Moses will accuse you! Yes, Moses, in whom you put your hopes." John 5:45 NLT

What Will The Verdict Be And What Does It Mean?

Judgment Day is when God reads the verdict for each one of us, based solely on the "evidence" we gave Him during our lifetime by the way we lived and the choices we made. The evidence is produced based upon the records of each individual's life, as recorded in "The Books." There will also be witnesses to further validate the perfect verdict. Here is how God describes this scene for us:

"Then I saw a great white throne and him who was seated on it. Earth and sky fled from his presence, and there was no place for them. And I saw the dead, great and small, standing

before the throne, and books were opened. Another book was opened, which is the book of life." Revelation 20:11-12 NIV

In our justice system, at the end of a trial, there is an air of suspense, anxiety, or anticipation while we wait for the verdict to be read. We have had some very famous trials over the past few decades, where people around the country stopped what they were doing and gathered around radios and televisions to hear the verdict being pronounced. There's also going to be a personal sense of suspense on Judgment Day, and for good reason.

As has been pointed out, this Day is not a trial but the time when God will simply pronounce each person's verdict and then separate them into two groups. Those on His right will be going to Heaven to live with Him, and those on His left will be thrown into the Lake of Fire (what we refer to as Hell) along with Satan and his fallen angels. The reason for the verdict is then given.

"All the nations will be gathered before him, and he will separate the people one from another as a shepherd separates the sheep from the goats. He will put the sheep on his right and the goats on his left. "Then [the Judge] will say to those on his right, 'Come, you who are blessed by my Father; take your inheritance, the kingdom prepared for you since the creation of the world.' "Then he will say to those on his left, 'Depart from me, you who are cursed, into the eternal fire prepared for the devil and his angels.' "Then they will go away to eternal punishment, but the righteous to eternal life." Matthew 25:32-34, 41 & 46 NIV

"This is the verdict: Light has come into the world,

About the goats He says:

"but men loved darkness instead of light because their deeds were evil. Everyone who does evil hates the light, and will not come into the light for fear that his deeds will be exposed."

About the sheep He says:

"But whoever lives by the truth comes into the light, so that it may be seen plainly that what he has done has been done through God." John 3:19-21 NIV

The goats are those who lived their lives avoiding, even rejecting God, never really seeking Him for fear what they are doing will become known. It's time for those individuals to realize that their fear and deeds will be revealed on this Day, so why not get before God and confess it now while there is still time to change their eternal destiny? On Judgment Day, even those who were religious and appeared to know Him will come to terms with the true state of their hearts. The following exhibits that even if you are a dedicated member in a religious group, or even a leader of a religion, it does not guarantee entrance into Heaven. Here are the words from God's own mouth:

"Not everyone who says to me, 'Lord, Lord,' will enter the kingdom of heaven, but only he who does the will of my Father who is in heaven. Many will say to me on that day, 'Lord, Lord, did we not prophesy in your name, and in your name drive out demons and perform many miracles?'" Matthew 7:21-22 NIV

Because He knows their hearts and motives, He knows that they never had a personal relationship with Him. He will respond:

"Then I will tell them plainly, 'I never knew you. Away from me, you evildoers!'" Matthew 7:23 NIV

On the other hand, the sheep are those whose actions proved their relationship with God. They come to God as a child comes to his or her father, and acknowledge they need Him to forgive them – to make their peace with Him.

Another dimension of what happens on Judgment day, along with the verdict, is that not everyone will be getting the same degree of reward or degree of punishment. In spite of there only being two groups of people, God recognizes that there will be differences in the severity of wrongs and the degree of good works. Accordingly, there will be degrees of punishment and rewards. Here's how God puts it:

> "But I tell you, it will be more bearable for Tyre and Sidon on the day of judgment than for you." Matthew 11:22 NIV

> "But I tell you that it will be more bearable for Sodom on the day of judgment than for you." Matthew 11:24 NIV

> "'See, your Savior comes! See, his reward is with him, and his recompense accompanies him.'" Isaiah 62:11 NIV

> "The time has come for judging the dead, and for rewarding your servants the prophets and your saints and those who reverence your name, both small and great" Revelation 11:18 NIV

> "The man who plants and the man who waters have one purpose, and each will be rewarded according to his own labor." 1 Corinthians 3:8 NIV

> "If what he has built survives, he will receive his reward." 1 Corinthians 3:14 NIV

This is a lot of new and surprising information for many reading this. It is information that is critical for each person to know and understand. Each one reading this is indeed without excuse. But most importantly, it is imperative for us to come to terms with the fact that only what we do in our lifetime will affect the outcome of that Day. There are no other opportunities – period.

What will you do with this information? What will your choice be? In the next chapter, we will be reading what exactly your choices are.

Chapter 6

Your Choice

Life is full of choices. We make choices every day, ranging from the very simple to the very complex; from the inconsequential to the ones that are life-changing. Having this freedom to choose is a gift from God that no one can take away from us, and God Himself will never violate. Each choice comes with its own set of consequences, whether they are good or bad.

The more life-impacting the choice we face, the more time we usually spend thinking about it. Some of the poorest decisions we make in life are the ones we don't take enough time to think through, by reflecting on how that choice will impact us and others who may be involved.

Choosing where we will spend eternity is the single most important and life-impacting choice anyone can make, as it determines where we will be for all eternity, with no opportunity to change our minds after we die.

What most people don't even realize is that this is a choice everyone makes, whether it is choosing to stay separated from God by not choosing to accept God's gift, or by taking the narrow road of escape He has put in front of everyone as an option. Ignoring the decision defaults to a choice of staying separated from God. It takes a definite decision to be saved from the eternal destiny of Hell, where everyone is headed unless they have entered into a personal relationship with God.

Making an informed choice of where we want to spend all eternity should involve time to think about the consequences of that decision. This is a decision of all or nothing – it is a commitment of the greatest magnitude we will ever face. Too many people avoid the subject because they would rather think about more pleasant things, and in most cases they are unaware of the facts. They are in effect trusting that God will take care of it all and everything will turn out right. When that is the case, we need to be a lot more proactive and put our trust in Him and our fate in His hands by acknowledging what He did that makes it possible for us to get to Heaven.

What Goes Into Making A Choice?

First, making a choice means there is more than one option or alternative. In the choice of where we spend eternity, God tells us there are only two choices. We are either choosing to go to Heaven by having a personal relationship with God as we read in the Chapter *Selection Criteria,* or we choose to stay separated from God and end up in the Lake of Fire. There are no other options.

The second step in making a choice is that we think about how the choice will impact us personally – weighing the benefits and the potential shortfalls. How we do this will vary by person, but when it comes to the critical choices, most people typically do some research and find out all they can before making the final decision.

The source and reliability of the facts as they relate to the choice you are about to make is critical. In this instance, the only source that matters is what God says, as He is the architect, creator and ultimate authority on the subject. The only reference in this book is what God tells us. God does not lie, He knows everything about us; He is perfect in every way. That means if anyone or anything contradicts what God tells us, we are being deceived. This is how seriously God will treat those who mislead people – He repeats Himself to emphasize just how serious this offense is:

> *"Let God's curses fall on anyone ... who preaches any other way to be saved than the one we told you about; yes, if an angel comes from heaven and preaches any other message,*

let him be forever cursed. I will say it again: if anyone preaches any other gospel than the one you welcomed, let God's curse fall upon him." Galatians 1:8-9 NLT

Something else we consider before making a choice of major importance is what others will think about us and how they will treat us – family, friends, neighbors, co-workers, fellow students, and people who we want as a part of our lives. In some societies, making a decision of this kind will be very impacting on our relationship with them. The thing to remember is that your relationship with God cannot come second to any other person, no matter who they are. Your relationship with God is eternal, your relationship with others is only a fleeting moment in comparison. Rest assured, no matter what pressure you may face in this decision, God promises it will not be more than you can handle. Here is His promise:

"No test or temptation that comes your way is beyond the course of what others have had to face. All you need to remember is that God will never let you down; he'll never let you be pushed past your limit; he'll always be there to help you come through it." 1 Corinthians 10:13 The Message

What Your Choice of Accepting God's Gift Means

Apart from Heaven just sounding like a place you would rather go than Hell, there are much more compelling reasons why God wants you to be with Him forever. The first thing we need to do in making the choice of wanting to be with God in Heaven, is to recognize that God is the only one who can save you from your current fate. After Jesus saw people stop following Him, he asked the ones who stayed if they would be leaving as well. They wisely responded:

"Lord, where would we go? You have the words that give eternal life. We believe and know that you are the Holy One from God." John 6:68-69 NCV

Even if you have been going to church all your life and really believe you will be going to Heaven when you die, take the time to make doubly sure. The question here is: "If you were to die today, where would you end up?" If you can't say with the deepest conviction, even pointing to a day when you accepted God's gift, there is too much room for doubt and it will be worth your time to reaffirm what you think you have already done.

When is the right time to make this decision? There's no time like right now, because we don't know how long we have before we draw our last breath. No one is promised tomorrow. There are too many tragic stories about children, teens, people in their prime of life who died unexpectedly. We never know if today will be our last, so delaying this decision is one of the worst choices you could possibly make. Why take a chance on the most important decision of your life? God has spoken to you:

"Today, if you hear his voice, do not harden your hearts" Heb 3:7-8 NIV

Right now He is knocking on the door of your heart:

"Here I am! I stand at the door and knock. If anyone hears my voice and opens the door, I will come in and eat with him, and he with me." Revelation 3:20 NIV

He's telling you the time is right now:

"I tell you, now is the time of God's favor, now is the day of salvation." 2 Corinthians 6:2 NIV

Don't procrastinate. This is something you could regret for all eternity. Remember, this choice has to be made while you are still alive. God has your attention right now. He has given you an ideal opportunity; He has been patient with you for many years:

"God is being patient with you. He does not want anyone to be lost, but he wants all people to change their hearts and lives." 2 Peter 3:9 NCV

Nobody else can make this choice for you. We can't ride on the "goodness" of someone else; we can't call on anyone else to get us into Heaven, as we learned from the account of the rich man and Lazarus. God is clear:

"You must choose for yourselves today whom you will serve." Josh 24:15 NCV

Make your choice to be with God forever, right now. Cry out to God, He will show Himself to you and prove who He is. Realize you need Him to rescue you from your current fate of eternal separation from Him in the Lake of Fire. This is exactly what God tells us we must do - acknowledge what He did for you to make it possible to get into Heaven:

- Thank Him for taking the punishment for your sins by dying on the cross
- He rose again on the third day as proof that HE conquered any grip death has on you
- Ask God to come into your heart now, answer the door, He's knocking
- Ask God to forgive you for all things that have kept you away from Him

If you made the choice of accepting God's gift of eternal life, welcome to God's family! Angels are rejoicing at your decision:

"I tell you, there is rejoicing in the presence of the angels of God over one sinner who repents." Luke 15:10 NIV

It's very important that you remember this day. It is in fact your spiritual birth date. Write your name in the box below, and the date.

You will always be able to turn to this page and confirm and reassure yourself that this is when you entered God's Kingdom.

Print/Sign Your Name   Date

So what just happened to you, and what does it mean to be a member of God's family? Let's read what God tells us.

First, you have been made brand new. You have been born spiritually from the Heavenly realms.

> "[You are] a new creation; the old has gone, the new has come! All this is from God, who reconciled us to himself through Christ." 2 Corinthians 5:17-18 NIV

God wiped your slate clean. God tells us He is choosing to forgive your sins of the past:

> "There is now no condemnation for those who are in Christ Jesus, because through Christ Jesus the law of the Spirit of life set me free from the law of sin and death." Romans 8:1-3 NIV

One thing to realize is – if you made this decision, all of your past mistakes are wiped clear from your slate – God is choosing to forget them and never to bring them up ever again.

> "He has removed our sins as far away from us as the east is from the west." Psalms 103:12 NLT

As member of God's family, you just became an heir to the riches in Heaven. Your name is in God's Book of Life, entitling you to inherit what God has set aside for you.

> "...we are [God's] children, then we are heirs — heirs of God and co-heirs with Christ." Romans 8:17 NIV

All of us who are members of His family should be thanking Him regularly for that wonderful benefit:

"... giving thanks to the Father, who has qualified you to share in the inheritance of the saints in the kingdom of light." Colossians 1:12 NIV

There is so much more. The best of which is the relationship we have with God. We will be able to approach Him with confidence. We have unlimited access to Him – anytime from anywhere.

Our relationships with others will take on new meaning as our interests will be aligned, focused on the eternal things of life.

The Last Chapter of this book *What Now?*, tells you about what you need to do, now that you are member of God's family. God gives us opportunities to build our relationship with Him, learn what our responsibilities are, and how we make ourselves available to Him to help others come into His Kingdom.

What Rejecting His Gift Means

By now you have read everything you need to know about what God says it takes to get into Heaven. It is very important to know that life totally separated from God is exponentially different than what life is now for you here on Earth. Even the most inhumane living conditions here are a paradise next to what it will be like in the Lake of Fire.

Many people think they will be able to live life pretty much the same as it is now. Nothing could be further from the truth. God tells us that those who choose to be separated from Him for all eternity will be THROWN into the Lake of Fire. They will be fighting as hard as they can to stay out, but will not be able to avoid their chosen destiny.

If you reject God's gift of eternal life with Him, the next couple of chapters may be what it takes to get your full attention and understand what your choice means to you, personally. If you choose to reject God's gift, what you are doing is choosing to stay separated from God, which means you are making the choice to go to Hell or more accurately, the Lake of Burning Sulfur. Before closing the door on God completely, it will be worth your time to read what God tells us what your existence will be like when completely separated from God.

Others believe they will be able to make their choice after they die. That's just wishful thinking with a fatal flaw. The moment people die, their eternal fate becomes instantly clear to them.

"If anyone's name was not found written in the book of life, he was thrown into the lake of fire." Rev 20:15 NIV

This is the perfect opportunity for you to accept God's gift. It may be your only opportunity. Don't let this moment slip away or take it lightly – seize the moment.

Chapter 7

Heaven

We now come to the focus of our desired end destination – Heaven. This is the eternal place that got your attention to pick up this book, for several possible reasons. First and foremost, you thought that is where you want to go when you die. The thought of death is not one we cherish, let alone something we care to think about. But we all will die one day, most folks are just not sure what happens at that point, and the fear of dying sets in to the point of us avoiding preparing for the inevitable departure from this world.

Make no mistake about it and have no doubts, something does happen right after your last breath. What most people hope, like when they cross their fingers, is that they will mysteriously end up in Heaven because they were "a good person." God tells us, even warns us, that nothing can be further from the truth.

We have already learned in the Chapter *Judgment Day* that there are only two possible destinations for all eternity. We also read in the Chapter *Selection Criteria* that there is only one way that we will be allowed to enter Heaven. If for some reason you missed that critical qualifier, you need to go back and understand God's standard, because getting to Heaven just doesn't happen by chance, it takes a deliberate choice on your part. In addition, we know from what God says in the Chapter *Your Choice*, that we are the only ones who can choose our ultimate destination. If you haven't made your decision yet, reading about Heaven may be the very thing that guides you to Heaven's Gates of Pearl.

After you read this Chapter, you may think, "Wow, what am I waiting for?" Or, you may decide, "If that's what it's going to be like, no thanks, I'm not interested." The next chapter may be a more convincing perspective for those who want to pass. This Chapter and the next one on Hell describe what life will be like in both places for all eternity.

Thinking About Heaven

God actually encourages us to spend time thinking about Heaven:

> "...set your hearts on things above [Heaven] ... Set your minds on things above, not on earthly things." Colossians 3:1,2 NIV

What is the point of thinking, or more importantly, setting your heart, on Heaven? You may be asking: "What good is that going to bring about? Besides, what do we know about Heaven that I could even spend more than a few minutes thinking about?" Great questions, and the answers will amaze you to the point where it should change the way you start each day and how you spend your time - eternally. It can be nothing less than life-changing.

Unfortunately, there are people who don't want to have anything to do with God. They do just about anything to walk away whenever anyone talks about God, and the thought of Heaven seems ridiculous. Heaven is probably the last place they want to be. If that is you, I hope you take the few minutes it takes to read this chapter and get a glimpse of what you are passing on. Then read the next chapter to see the only other option.

Then there are people who have a heartfelt desire to know and be with God. This desire can be likened to wanting to go home – for some reason, we know there is a better place than where we are. These folks are longing for that better place to live. Here is how that desire is described in the Bible:

"... they were longing for a better country — a Heavenly one. Therefore God is not ashamed to be called their God, for he has prepared a city for them." Hebrews 11:16 NIV

God responds to that longing for a better place by actually preparing one for those who want to make Heaven their home. People who meet God's criteria by entering into a personal relationship with Him are the only ones who will walk through the Gates of Heaven. There is more to Heaven than just getting there; you are a "citizen," with all of the privileges and responsibilities associated with citizenship. That citizenship actually starts here on Earth after we make our peace with God. God affirms that notion for us:

"But we are citizens of heaven, where the Lord Jesus Christ lives. And we are eagerly waiting for him to return as our Savior." Philippians 3:20 NLT

Heaven fulfills our hope for a better place, and we can have total confidence that we will indeed be going when we understand God's ways and willingly choose to be a part of all that God has planned. God's desire is for everyone to want to spend eternity in relationship with Him – that's how He designed us, and as we said earlier, we are the only ones who can make that choice. God guarantees Heaven as the destination, for those who make that choice according to His criteria. And for those who choose to make their peace with God, He reassures that nothing will prevent that from happening:

"Now it is God who has made us for this very purpose and has given us the Spirit as a deposit, guaranteeing what is to come." 2 Corinthians 5:5 NIV

To better understand Heaven from our current reality, it may help to give an example of something many people may have dreamt about or done. For example, like going on a long-awaited dream vacation. Did you ever plan or even think about such a vacation to a place you always wanted to visit? A place you had never seen or visited before? Do you remember what you imaged it was going to be like when you got there? Our imaginations can be pretty amazing, and it may have taken you to the outer limits of what the place could possibly be like.

Then, the closer you came to the date of your departure, the more excited you became, and the anticipation of all your expectations grew. What made it that much more intriguing was talking about the trip with the one(s) who were going with you. Sometimes these trips turn out to be real disappointments, major letdowns; other times they are all you imagined them to be and more – producing memories you will always cherish. Well, going to Heaven has many of the same overtones. Only it's infinitely different from many perspectives.

The first difference that comes to mind, between a dream vacation and the journey to Heaven, is how you get there. A few of those thoughts are:

- It's easy to think about our methods of transportation – car, plane, train, boat; but the getting to Heaven is an entirely different mode of transportation. Angels take you up at no charge, without any delays.
- Then there is the actual cost of the trip. When we go on vacation, we usually have to work long and hard to pay for the trip. Very few people can just make the decision to go, pack, and leave with little or no planning. Going to this dream destination is something anyone who has the money can do. Going to Heaven costs us nothing – it's a gift we only have to choose to accept. God doesn't let us in because we are better than most people – you have to have that personal relationship with Him. He has to know you.
- As for the imagination of what to expect on a dream vacation, we could just about exhaust the realm of possibilities. When it comes to Heaven, you will never come close to exhausting all the possibilities.

Let's move on and see what Heaven is like. The first thing is that most will be surprised that Heaven as it currently exists is different from the one that will be in place later.

Current Heaven

Very few people realize that there is a difference between what Heaven is like now, and what it will be like at the end of this age. Yes, even Heaven has a before and after picture, because things will be vastly better when everything is finally set in place for all eternity. To see the differences, let's get into what the current Heaven looks like. Here is the account God gives us as it relates to one individual, Lazarus, as an example to us. You may remember him as the one in the account of the rich man:

> "Then he died, this poor man, and was taken up by the angels to the lap of Abraham...here he's consoled..." Luke 16:22,25 The Message

Here is Lazarus, who went from a very miserable life while he was alive on Earth to his promised place in Heaven. Lazarus in paradise is released from all the misery he was in. Jesus referred to the current Heaven as paradise, as we see from the account of when Jesus made a promise to one of the thieves who was being crucified next to Him. Starting with what the thief said:

> "Then he said, 'Jesus, remember me when you enter your kingdom.' He said, 'Don't worry, I will. Today you will join me in paradise.'" Luke 23:42-43 The Message

One difference between the current Heaven and the one to come is that those who are in the present Heaven can see the people who are in Hell. That will not be the case when the New Heaven is put in place. Expanding on the account of Lazarus, God tells us about the proximity of Heaven and Hell:

> "Then he died, this poor man, and was taken up by the angels to the lap of Abraham. The rich man also died and was buried. In hell and in torment, he looked up and saw Abraham in the distance and Lazarus in his lap. He called out, 'Father Abraham, mercy! Have mercy! Send Lazarus to

dip his finger in water to cool my tongue. I'm in agony in this fire.'" Luke 16:22-24 The Message

From the current Heaven (paradise), one can see those on the other side (Hell) being held for the Day of Judgment. One does not need a lot of time to realize that seeing others in torment would hardly be a state of peace and tranquility. In the New Heaven, we will not be able to see those who are in Hell. In the current Heaven, there is also an impenetrable barrier between the two places. Reading more about what God tells us about the current Heaven:

"But Abraham said, 'Child, remember that in your lifetime you got the good things and Lazarus the bad things. It's not like that here. Here he's consoled and you're tormented. Besides, in all these matters there is a huge chasm set between us so that no one can go from us to you even if he wanted to, nor can anyone cross over from you to us.'" Luke 16:25-26 The Message

As nice as Heaven is now, spending more time on what the current Heaven is like would be like dwelling on a layover on your trip while going to your final destination. Suffice it to say, the current Heaven is a much better place than where we are currently, no matter how good you may have it. In the next chapter, we will read how *Hell* is worse than anything anyone is experiencing now.

All that we know and can see now will no longer exist as we know it, because God will be making everything new. The present Heaven will be replaced by the New Heaven and the New Earth on Judgment Day.

New Heaven and New Earth

"Then I saw a new heaven and a new earth, for the first heaven and the first earth had passed away..." Revelation 21:1 NIV

OK, we now know the present heaven and Earth will no longer exist in their current state. However, the Greek word "New" God uses here tells us God will be re-creating both Heaven and Earth, not wiping them out of existence. That means we will be back on this same planet, totally purged of any imperfections – both materially, and with those who will be living here. In essence, the New Heaven includes the New Earth and more accurately, the entire universe!

So just what is the New Heaven going to be like? The reality of Heaven is so wonderful, so beautiful and magnificent, that our human minds and imaginations cannot fully take it in. Our languages are incapable of describing it. Let's see what God tells us we can look forward to:

"No eye has seen, no ear has heard, no mind has conceived what God has prepared for those who love him" – 1 Cor 2:9 NIV

Just think about it, God is telling us there is no way we can imagine what it's going to be like in Heaven, no matter how hard we try. I don't know about you, but I have a pretty vivid imagination. So much so, that many times I am disappointed by the reality of what happens versus what I was hoping would happen. We don't even have the capacity to imagine it – it is actually in the realm of the impossible.

As a vivid contrast to help us realize the awesomeness of Heaven, God tells us that the best this life has to offer is like a shadow compared to what is coming. Imagine living in a world made up of nothing but shadows – one-dimensional, colorless, tasteless – and compare that to the best this world has to offer. That means that the most vivid, wonderful experiences we can ever have engaging all our senses and emotions is a one-dimensional, black-and-white, lifeless shadow compared to what God has prepared for us in Heaven. Even that contrast falls infinitely short of the contrast between Earth and Heaven. Here is the way God put it:

"[the splendor of our present world]... These are a shadow of the things that were to come..." Colossians 2:17 NIV

The fact is, we long not only to see what Heaven will be like as a place, but we also want to know what the future life there will be like. God tells us that even the angels long to see these things themselves, and they already have a better vantage point of view:

"... Even angels long to look into these things." 1 Pet 1:12 NIV

It's important also for us to also realize that as much as we may be looking forward to getting to Heaven, God is looking forward to us being with Him. So much so that He says it over and again throughout the Bible. Here are two of the many references. The first instance below is from the present standpoint, where God is looking forward to that time, and the second from the perspective of when we are finally with him in Heaven:

"My dwelling place will be with them; I will be their God, and they will be my people." Ezekiel 37:27 NIV

"... Now the dwelling of God is with men, and he will live with them. They will be his people, and God himself will be with them and be their God." Revelation 21:3 NIV

I know what it's like to wait to see dear ones after being separated for long periods of time – you just can't wait to be with them again. When I was a young child, we used to go to the airport to meet my dad when he returned from a business trip. I missed having him home with us, and wanted to see him as soon as I possibly could. We should have this same sense of longing and anticipation about Heaven.

Heaven is indeed a place where we will live. And if we are going to be living there with God, we will need a place to stay. Just as a perfect Father would have it, He is preparing a special place for everyone who makes the choice:

> *"In my Father's house are many rooms; if it were not so, I would have told you. I am going there to prepare a place for you." John 14:2 NIV*

> *"... we have a building from God, an eternal house in Heaven, not built by human hands." 2 Corinthians 5:1 NIV*

This is by far better than anything we have ever seen or could imagine. Bigger and better than the Taj Mahal or any other mansion or castle ever built.

Another great aspect of Heaven is that so many of the things that make life here unpleasant, even painful, will disappear. God tell us:

> *"He will wipe every tear from their eyes, and there will be no more death or sorrow or crying or pain. All these things are gone forever." Revelation 21:4 NLT*

Tears come from two sources – physical pain and emotional pain. God is telling neither of these will be found in Heaven — they will be gone FOREVER — from the most insignificant discomfort to the most unbearable pain and agony. You won't even stub your toe, nor have one moment of conflict with anyone! I have both friends and family members who have physical, emotional and intellectual limitations. God tells us those who choose to go to Heaven will be fully restored. What a great transformation for them. Go ahead, think about anything in your life that you would want to change from this perspective. What would Heaven include or exclude in your life?

Yes, God tells us that the old way is gone and He is starting all over:

> *"... the old order of things has passed away ... I am making everything new!" Revelation 21:4, 5 NIV*

Let's keep going here, so we can help the imagination to at least try to get an appreciation for what God is preparing for those of us who choose to be with Him.

From the physical standpoint, everything unpleasant involving our five senses will go away. From an emotional standpoint, we will no longer weep or cry. God is wiping the slate clean and starting over. He is making everything new. Heaven is perfect in every imaginable way, ranging from the things that will be there to the people who will be living there.

Heaven is a place absent of the toils, pains, sufferings, and sorrows that we often experience in our lives. We long for relief from these unwelcome experiences that distract us from enjoying life to its fullest here on Earth. These things are not just unpleasant, they keep us from reaching our full potential. We don't grow the way we were designed to grow; we don't think or use our brains to the fullest. Every aspect of our being is stunted here on Earth. In Heaven, we will have the freedom to explore and grow, do the things we always wanted to do but couldn't because of our circumstances.

Let's look at a broader perspective of life in Heaven. This is all part of "setting our minds on things above," and will give us food for thought so we can be inspired by just how much God loves us and is preparing for us. In return, we should be moved to do everything we should and can to show God our gratitude, by living our lives the way He tells us is best for us and those around us.

Life in Heaven is made up of both the physical/material and relational, so let's look at a list of what will be changing in each as part of our new lives in Heaven. Instead of going into depth with each one, I challenge you to think of each one and what you think they will be like.

Unfortunately, when people think about what Heaven will be like, we think almost exclusively about its physical attributes. That's understandable, since we are very focused on the material world around us. Most of us have heard about the streets of gold, the pearly gates, etc. Now that is all good and well, but it is only the "garnish" of the real wonder of Heaven.

On the physical and material side, here are some of things we can explore:

- New bodies – perfect in every way, never aging or breaking down, all our senses working perfectly at levels we don't even know about (sounds, sight, touch, taste, smell).
- New clothes – brilliant, reflecting our character and purpose, never wearing out, never out of style.
- New homes – paid for in full, fully equipped and furnished, everything working to perfection, everything we need.
- New food – tastes that you never knew existed, providing the pleasure and nourishment we need and want (not sure about the calories!)
- New dimensions – there will be expanded laws of physics, depths, breadths, heights.
- New modes of getting from place to place – Teleporting, flying?

Let's go a little further in depth about our bodies, as this gets as personal as anything we are currently familiar with. God tells us we are going to get new bodies! Not just ones that resemble what we had at its best here on Earth, but a new and improved "model." I'm looking forward to that – the older I get, the more I see the need for that, as I can no longer do the things I used to do when I was in my prime – or at least not nearly as well. Knees crack, vision is deteriorating, and hearing is going. You get the idea. Many people are obsessed with trying to stop the aging process, and spend untold dollars in the process of trying to stay young looking. The fact is, we all get older and eventually die. There is no fountain of youth down here.

So what does God tell us about these new bodies? Let's read:

"If there is a natural body, there is also a spiritual body. ... flesh and blood cannot inherit the kingdom of God, nor does the perishable inherit the imperishable. Listen, I tell you a mystery: ...we will all be changed ... the dead will be raised imperishable, and we will be changed. For the perishable must clothe itself with the imperishable, and the mortal with immortality." 1 Corinthians 15:44-54 NIV

Also,

> "... by the power that enables him to bring everything under his control, will transform our lowly bodies so that they will be like his glorious body." Philippians 3:20-21 NIV

That means that our bodies are going to be perfect in every way. We will never age, we will never get sick, never be overweight, nor have any abnormalities, just totally completely perfect. This already sounds too good to be true, but since I can imagine this, we aren't even scratching the surface of just how good it gets. I get excited just thinking about it!

Another proof that we will be getting these new bodies is this recording of when Jesus came back in His new, glorious body:

> "On the evening of that first day of the week, when the disciples were together, with the doors locked for fear of the Jews, Jesus came and stood among them and said, 'Peace be with you!' After he said this, he showed them his hands and side." John 20:19-20 NIV

This account shows us that Jesus did not need to go through any door to get in the room. That is obviously something very different than what we are limited in doing right now. Another account of what we will be able to do in our new bodies is illustrated here:

> "It was not long afterwards that he rose into the sky and disappeared into a cloud, leaving them staring after him. As they were straining their eyes for another glimpse, suddenly two white-robed men were standing there among them, and said, 'Men of Galilee, why are you standing here staring at the sky? Jesus has gone away to heaven, and some day, just as he went, he will return!'" Acts 1:9-11 NLT

Rising into the sky! We will be able to fly away to various places. No need to get the car, bike, cab or whatever. No breakdowns or fuel cost, either. You can see how just a few of these accounts can get us thinking about what is to come.

God tells us that we will be getting new "clothes" as well. Our bodies are going to be clothed in God's best, in a sense, Heaven's "designer clothes":

> *"She has been given the finest of pure white linen to wear. For the fine linen represents the good deeds of God's holy people." Revelation 19:8 NLT*

The interesting part here is we are the ones who determine what we are going to wear, by how obedient we are to God's commands after we have been reconciled to Him. This is how we spin our own threads, from the treasures we lay up in Heaven.

As enamored as we get with the material side of life – what we wear, where we live, what we drive – the best part of Heaven will be our relationships. That is the real substance of what the New Heaven is all about.

Our relationship with God will be totally open and unencumbered – none of the current barriers that make God seem so far away. We will be able to see His "face," and hear His voice in such a way that we will understand everything He says and exactly what He means. Our relationship with Him and others will reach new depths and substance, bringing such an intimate relationship that we will be one - one in purpose, one in being. No arguing, no hidden agendas, no turmoil or arguing EVER. Now, that is beyond our understanding. I have a hard enough time just agreeing with myself at times, but being one with everyone else at the same time is too hard to take in.

The relational part of life is much more complex. Just as we did for the material side of life in Heaven, we have a list that brushes the realm of relationships. This list has more room for the imagination, but the ones we list here should make us want to be in Heaven more than any of the physical or material part of Heaven.

- Perfect family and friends – reunited with family members and friends, making new friends

- New minds, thoughts and memories – thinking clearly and in a healthy manner regarding your relationships with others, sharing experiences together, doing things together
- New desires – constructive and edifying
- New emotions – balanced and strong, no mood swings
- New jobs and responsibilities – doing what you love doing and being excellent at what you do
- New skills – doing new things better than ever and always improving
- New learning – wanting to learn more about everything in depth and fully understanding the truth
- New plans and dreams – expanded realms and possibilities (the universe is a big place!)
- New expanded language and vocabulary – everyone will understand what you say and mean, no miscommunications or barriers

Go ahead, use your imagination, and make your own list. You will never exhaust the possibilities.

Since life in Heaven is mostly about relationships, let's take a little more time here to explore what these relationships will be like. This is more challenging, in that using our imaginations on what the material part of Heaven will be like comes a little easier to most of us. We will see just why there will be no more tears, pain, crying or dying, when we understand what God is changing in this part of our lives.

As I pointed out above, we will never have any arguments or disagreements with each other. No one will be doing anything out of selfishness, everyone will be honest, kind, patient, and loving in everything we do and at all times. We will love being with others and in complete harmony. There won't even be a hint of jealousy, nor will we be suspicious of others. We will trust everyone implicitly. Nothing we do will contradict or undermine what others are doing. Everyone will be working together for the same purposes and with the same pure motives. There won't be any cheating, stealing, lying, malice, perversion, hatred, manipulating or anything else you can think of that would make life less than perfect. I don't know about you, but I just can't imagine what that would be like, all the time without any lapses.

Another dimension of relationships is seen in what we will be doing in Heaven. We're not going to be sitting on clouds, strumming harps all day long. We will have responsibilities – a job, so to speak, that fits us to perfection. We will be fulfilled, appreciated, productive, skilled, as well as happy, and all at the same time in everything we do.

So what sort of jobs will there be in heaven? Since God does not give us a lot of insight into that part of life in Heaven, it may be easier to start with the professions that will no longer be needed. In keeping with God's promise of there being no more pain or suffering, there obviously won't be a need for doctors, lawyers, military, banks, or police, to name a few. It also means there won't be any jails, hospitals, or slums. And since life will be very different in Heaven on how we will be getting around, there won't be any need for cars, airplanes, trains and the like.

So what will we be doing? What we can be sure of is that God gives each one of us unique talents – we see those talents in people now, where individuals show something that just seems to come naturally to them almost without trying. It's like it's a part of who they are, and as a bonus, they love using that talent. Talents like to singing, playing an instrument, building, cooking, painting, and there are a multitude of others. Whatever our talents will be in Heaven, they will be at levels beyond what we have ever experienced, and doing it to perfection. You will have a job you love and you will be excellent at what you do.

Again, I challenge you to think about anything else in life that would fit into what would make up a perfect Heaven. No matter what you come up with, God says it's going to be extremely better than anything you dream up! It should go without saying, but only the activities that fit with God's perfect character will be happening in Heaven. Once we get to Heaven, we wouldn't want anything else anyway, but while we are still down here, we need to remind ourselves of what would and wouldn't be acceptable.

All of what we just went through fits in with what God will be providing us once we get there. There is actually something we can do now to influence and affect what will be waiting for us when we finally arrive. It's kind of a Heavenly savings account.

Preparing Now for Heaven

The more you know about Heaven, the more you can prepare for it. God tells us that what we do here on Earth will have a great deal to do with what you can expect in Heaven. As awesome as we have seen what Heaven will be like, the substance of that abundance will largely depend on what we do after we have made our peace with God, and do for Him out of love and unselfish ambition.

In our lives we have talents, possessions and relationships with others. Once we have a personal relationship with God, He expects us to use what we have for His ultimate purposes and not hoard them. When we do this, God tells us that we are storing up rewards in Heaven that we will one day inherit.

God tells us that when we hoard or work for material possessions for the here and now, we are putting our energies onto things that will be burned up and destroyed at some point. He also tells us that when we live our lives according to His plan for our lives, we are storing up treasures in Heaven. In fact, the very things we can expect to find in Heaven come under three topics – treasures, rewards, and an inheritance. Here is God's advice summarizing this:

> *"Don't hoard treasure down here where it gets eaten by moths and corroded by rust or — worse! — stolen by burglars. Stockpile treasure in heaven, where it's safe from moth and rust and burglars. It's obvious, isn't it? The place where your treasure is, is the place you will most want to be, and end up being." Matt 6:19-21 the Message*

Just what are these treasures? As any loving Father would do, He gives us insight into what we can do now to gather and store up these treasures. The first "ingredient" is that of faith in God. Faith is what qualifies any of these treasures for the Heavenly storehouse, for without it all we are doing is exerting energy needlessly. Here is what God says:

"And without faith it is impossible to please God, because anyone who comes to him must believe that he exists and that he rewards those who earnestly seek him." Heb 11:6 NIV

An example of what we can do that will qualify as a deposit in our treasury is giving:

"...so that your giving may be in secret. Then your Father, who sees what is done in secret, will reward you." Matt 6:4 NIV

Most people default to the giving of money, and that is one of the ways to give, but what God includes in the realm of giving involves our time, actually investing in people to bring them into a better relationship with God. We are also to share what we have. All of our possessions ultimately belong to God, and we are just custodians who are responsible for their use. Another example of how we store up treasures in heaven is illustrated here for us by God, with the focus of what we do with what God gives us:

"A nobleman living in a certain province was called away to the distant capital of the empire to be crowned king of his province. Before he left he called together ten assistants and gave them each $2,000 to invest while he was gone. But some of his people hated him and sent him their declaration of independence, stating that they had rebelled and would not acknowledge him as their king. Upon his return he called in the men to whom he had given the money, to find out what they had done with it, and what their profits were. The first man reported a tremendous gain - ten times as much as the original amount! 'Fine!' the king exclaimed. 'You are a good man. You have been faithful with the little I entrusted to you, and as your reward, you shall be governor of ten cities.' The next man also reported a splendid gain - five times the original amount. 'All right!' his master said. 'You can be governor over five cities.' But the third man brought back only the money he had started with. 'I've kept it safe,' he said,

'because I was afraid [you would demand my profits], for you are a hard man to deal with, taking what isn't yours and even confiscating the crops that others plant.' 'You vile and wicked slave,' the king roared. 'Hard, am I? That's exactly how I'll be toward you! If you knew so much about me and how tough I am, then why didn't you deposit the money in the bank so that I could at least get some interest on it?' Then turning to the others standing by he ordered, 'Take the money away from him and give it to the man who earned the most.' 'But, sir,' they said, 'he has enough already!' 'Yes,' the king replied, 'but it is always true that those who have, get more, and those who have little, soon lose even that.'" Luke 19:12-26 NLT

And when do we get these rewards? Quite obviously, when we get to Heaven:

"Behold, I am coming soon! My reward is with me, and I will give to everyone according to what he has done. Revelation 22:12 NIV

These treasures and rewards are what God calls our inheritance, which He is holding for us in Heaven:

"You will receive an inheritance from the Lord as a reward." Colossians 3:24 NIV

"He has given us new birth into a living hope ... and into an inheritance that can never perish, spoil or fade — kept in heaven for you" 1 Peter 1:3-5 NIV

I remember when Howard Hughes, one of the world's wealthiest men at the time, died. Many people tried to figure ways of inheriting even a small portion of the billions he left behind. Even if they had succeeded in inheriting the entire estate, it would have been petty cash and insignificant next to the smallest rewards we will receive in Heaven.

Have you made your peace with God, being reconciled to Him and in a personal relationship with Him? If not, nothing you have done that even appears noble counts toward the rewards in Heaven. Don't waste any more of your life, and get right with God so you can begin storing up these treasures as part of your inheritance, never mind the significance of making sure you end up in Heaven. No one knows how long they will be around.

Even with this brief overview, it doesn't take long to realize that Heaven is real and an incredible place, better than anything anyone can imagine. Who in their right minds wouldn't want this to be their future home? The sad thing is, there are people who would rather forego Heaven. What they may not know is that the only other alternative may not be what they had in mind. Brace yourself because the next Chapter, *Hell*, is as terrifying as Heaven is awesome.

Chapter 8

Hell

There was a song in the sixties made popular by Blood Sweat and Tears, written by Laura Nyro entitled "And When I Die" with the following lyrics:

> *"I can swear there ain't no Heaven*
> *but I pray there ain't no hell*
> *Swear there ain't no Heaven*
> *and I'll pray there ain't no hell*
> *but I'll never know by livin'*
> *only my dyin' will tell, yes only my*
> *dyin' will tell, oh yeah,*
> *Only my dyin' will tell."*

These lyrics bring out an interesting irony. It declares an absolute stand on knowing that Heaven does not exist, yet hopes that Hell is just a figment of the imagination. A seemingly pretty safe approach to the afterlife on the surface – if they are wrong about heaven, there is only gain; if they are wrong about Hell, they leave the door open for a possible appeal based on ignorance, as only their dying will let them know that Hell is real. The tragedy of this approach is it will be too late at that point to do anything about their eternal destiny.

But why should anyone wait until they die to find out, especially with such dire consequences? In the previous Chapter, we read what

God tells us about the reality of Heaven. In this Chapter, we will read about what God tells us about the reality of Hell.

Why Is There A Hell?

The very concept of Hell is probably a little harder to understand than Heaven, because it doesn't seem to fit in with God's character. How could a loving God send anyone to a place like Hell? Interestingly enough, God never intended for there to be a Hell. It's a place He had to prepare after Lucifer (better known as Satan) and the other fallen angels (better known as demons) decided to separate themselves from God to pursue their own selfish ambitions. Here is what God tells us happened that caused Him to prepare a place for those who chose not to be with Him:

"And the angels who did not keep their positions of authority but abandoned their own home ..." Jude 1:6 NIV

"...God did not spare angels when they sinned, but sent them to hell." 2 Peter 2:4 NIV

"...prepared for the devil and his angels" Matt 25:41 NIV

Unfortunately, mankind made the same decision to sever their relationship with God. Let's revisit what we read in *Who am I?*:

"Have you eaten from the tree that I commanded you not to eat from?" Gen 3:11 NIV

"So the Lord God banished him from the Garden of Eden" Genesis 3:23 NIV

God cannot "live" in the same place as individuals who are not able to have a perfect relationship – disobedience is sin, which causes immediate separation from God. This is what compelled God to prepare a place for those who, in effect, have to be separated from Him. Don't be deceived, Hell is a real place prepared by God because of our choice.

What Is Hell Like?

So what is a place without God like? Right now God's grace, or favor, falls upon all of us, whether we hate Him or love Him. That's right; God is being very merciful and patient with everyone because it's His desire for all of us to be with Him in Heaven forever. You may ask, "How is God's grace showing up in my life? I don't see it or even know what that means."

Let's examine just how God's grace shows up in our lives. First, let's look at the physical realm. We are alive, we breath and we have a heartbeat – none of which we started or continue to do on our own by our own will. There is no way you or anyone else can make sure that these functions continue for as long as you want; they are all gifts from God. Then there is the sun that shines, the rain that falls, and the air we breathe, regardless of our relationship with God. It has nothing to do with your stature in life, what religion you belong to, where you live, or any other circumstance. These are the things we see and experience daily; things that no one controls or pours out, other than God by His grace and mercy. Life for most is pretty good when it comes to these parts of life.

Then there are the spiritual and emotional realms of our lives. In the spiritual realm, God tells us the consequence of our choices outside of what it takes to have a full relationship with Him is death. Read what God said to Adam as He warns him of those consequences:

> *"You are free to eat from any tree in the garden; but you must not eat from the tree of the knowledge of good and evil, for when you eat of it you will surely die." Genesis 2:16-17 NIV*

God is not just talking about physical death here. The primary death is a relational one – the choice to go outside the boundaries God set for Adam will kill their relationship. All of the benefits of having a pure and whole relationship with God will come to an end. The grace part is that the death is not instant, God remains patient with us. Unfortunately, all too often we deceive ourselves to believe that His patience is really that we got away with something, or that what God said was not true.

In the last Chapter, we talked about Heaven as the ultimate perfect home God has prepared for each one of us who want to be with Him forever. Heaven contains the fullness of God without any hindrance. Hell is just the opposite. It's a place totally devoid of God's grace and mercy. All of the things that people take for granted, as we identified above, will no longer be available to the people who don't want to be with God. In Heaven, you get all that comes with being with God; in Hell, you do completely away with all that comes with God.

"OK, so Hell is a real place," you may concede, "but just how bad can it be?" I have often heard people say, "I'll just be with all my friends, and we can party together." What they don't understand is that the quality of life for them will not continue as it did before. So in effect, the grace they benefit from and take for granted will change dramatically in Hell, in the realm away from God.

Yet just as we discovered about Heaven, the current Hell is not the final destination for those who will be separated from God for all eternity – that place, we are told by God, is called the Lake of Fire or Lake of Burning Sulfur. Both names personify the unimaginable pain and torment of such a place. Let's see what God tells us about what Hell is like now and what it will be like as the Lake of Burning Sulfur.

Current Hell

The term Hell is a pretty universal one. You don't have to explain much of what you mean when referring to Hell, people seem to instinctively know it's a "bad" place. God confirms that notion when He shares what Hell feels like in the account we read about earlier in the book, about Lazarus and the rich man. Let's just take another look at the part where the rich man describes his state of being in Hell.

*"In hell, where he (the rich man) was in torment, he looked up and saw Abraham far away, with Lazarus by his side. So he called to him, 'Father Abraham, have pity on me and send Lazarus to dip the tip of his finger in water and cool my tongue, because I am in **agony** in this fire.'" Luke 16:23-24 NIV*

The rich man tells us he is in agony, or as the word in the original language implies, torture. The Greek word used here for tormented translates more clearly to torture, which the dictionary defines as the act of inflicting excruciating [extremely painful, intense suffering, unbearably distressing] pain in both body and mind. This intense and excruciating pain he is experiencing is both physical and mental. We talked about God's grace earlier and how it stops when in Hell. This story illustrates what life is like in the absence of God's grace. There is no healing or end to this agony, it continues and never ends. There is never any relief.

God also tells us that Hell is also where demons are being held until after Judgment Day:

"God didn't spare angels who sinned. He threw them into hell, where he has secured them with chains of darkness and is holding them for judgment." 2 Peter 2:4 NIV

Another way God gives each one of us a glimpse of what Hell will be like is through our own life experiences. Take a moment and think of the most severe physical pain you have ever experienced. Now couple that experience with the most painful emotional trauma in your life. Do you remember the pain you felt? You may have cried out that you couldn't take it any longer. That degree of pain is a small fraction of what Hell is like. This is obviously a place no one would want to end up in for all eternity.

Yet so many people on the path that leads to Hell, or eternal death, don't even realize it. Each person has to make their own choice to get on the path of eternal life. God tells us that the path to Hell is anything that does not bring us into perfect relationship with Him:

> *"For wide is the gate and broad is the road that leads to destruction, and many enter through it."* Matthew 7:13 NIV

As "bad" as the current Hell is, it is a temporary place that will be consumed by one that is an even worse place. God tells us that Hell will be thrown into Lake of Burning Sulfur at the end of Judgment Day.

> *"Then death and [Hell] were thrown into the lake of fire."* Revelation 20:14 NIV

How much worse can the Lake of Burning Sulfur be than Hell? Let's see what God tells us.

Lake Of Burning Sulfur

The name "Lake of Burning Sulfur" is in and of itself pretty descriptive as a place of torment. I remember being burned a few times in my life, and the pain is the worst physical pain I've ever experienced because it is so penetrating and lingers for such a long time. One instance in particular was when I struck a match and the sulfur tip of the match ignited and imbedded itself in my finger. It seemed like nothing I tried to stop the pain worked, it just kept getting worse, and actually burned a small hole in my finger. Even though that was a long time ago, the memory is still pretty vivid.

As bad as pain can be, most of us tolerate and get through it better because we know that in time, the pain will go away. The following passage tells us that in the Lake of Burning Sulfur, there is no end to the agony. How devastating it will be, just knowing that there will never be any relief from the excruciating pain – hopelessness beyond our comprehension.

> *"The smoke of their torment will rise forever and ever, and they will have no relief day or night."* Revelation 14:11 NLT

When the rich man was in Hell, he could see Abraham and Lazarus. That means there is some light in the existing Hell. I've been to several countries that were so remote, in the middle of the night, it was so dark you couldn't see your hand right in front of your face. The pitch-black darkness was so real you could almost feel it, like being immersed in a sea of darkness. The longer I was in that darkness, the more I felt smothered, and all I wanted to do was get somewhere where there was light. God tells us that in the Lake of Burning Sulfur, there won't be any light:

"...They are doomed to blackest darkness." 2 Peter 2:17 NLT

Apart from the physical torment that will be ever present, there will also be extreme pain or anguish of the mind and emotions. Comparatively speaking, mental torment is often worse than the physical pain. In the Lake of Burning Sulfur, the emotional pain will be so intense people will be screaming and gritting their teeth.

"They will throw them into the fiery furnace, where there will be weeping and gnashing of teeth." Matthew 13:42 NIV

The Lake of Burning Sulfur is a place where misery is ever present. This is the eternal dwelling of people confined to the society of the devil, demons, and wicked men. It is a place where there are uncontrolled passions and ungratified desires. There is the full realization that people are unable to escape or obtain relief; it is everlasting, forever, for all eternity.

Those in the Lake of Burning Sulfur have the sense that they are always dying, and yet they never die. The agony a person is in is so intense that he would think he is dying every moment, and yet he continues to live.

"...thrown into hell, where 'their worm does not die, and the fire is not quenched.' Everyone will be salted with fire." Mark 9:47-49 NIV

Being thrown into the Lake of Burning Sulfur is called the second death, which is a death different from the common and natural. This death destroys a person's well-being, but not his being; his happiness or contentment, but not his substance.

Some people may say that they don't want to be with God, but they don't want to go to Hell, either. These individuals need to come to terms with the fact that God tells us that there are no other choices; it's either Heaven or the Lake of Burning Sulfur. At the Last Judgment, those who are going to spend eternity in the Lake of Burning Sulfur come to realize the conditions of that place and fight as hard as they can to stay out. God gives us a glimpse of the time immediately before they reach their final destination:

> "...their fate is in the fiery lake of burning sulfur. This is the second death." Revelation 21:8 NLT

> "But the beast was captured, and with him the false prophet who had performed the miraculous signs on his behalf.... The two of them were thrown alive into the fiery lake of burning sulfur." Revelation 19:20 NIV

> "Then the devil, who had deceived them, was thrown into the fiery lake of burning sulfur, joining the beast and the false prophet. There they will be tormented day and night forever and ever." Revelation 20:10 NLT

These scenes are ones of extreme violence, as these individuals are thrown into the Lake of Burning Sulfur because they do not willingly go. They made their choice in where they will spend eternity.

What Is God Doing To Help You Escape Hell?

God knows the full reality and devastation of the Lake of Burning Sulfur and is doing His part to prevent people from defaulting to that destiny – He warns:

> *"You can enter God's Kingdom only through the narrow gate. The highway to hell is broad, and its gate is wide for the many who choose that way."* Matt 7:13-14 NLT

He is getting His message across to you in many ways. God uses people to take this message to us. He will use circumstances and any other means to get our attention. He is faithful and persistent, because He loves you and wants you to be reconciled to Him and spend eternity with Him in Heaven.

He doesn't want to scare you into Heaven by telling you how bad it is in Hell. God doesn't do that any more than you can scare somebody into a relationship. God leaves the decision to you alone as to whether or not you see and acknowledge what He has done to make a way out of the path of destruction you are on.

Not only is God constantly working to save you, but there is another "force" at work to make sure you don't escape the destiny of Hell.

What Is Satan Doing To Make Sure You Go To Hell?

Just as God is doing everything to show us we need to choose to make our peace with Him and have a relationship with Him, Satan is determined and consumed with trying to make sure you end up separated from God for all eternity. God describes Satan as a roaring lion, out to kill and destroy as many people as he can by deceiving you and anyone else he can. God warns us that our enemy, Satan, is coming after you:

> *"Your enemy the devil prowls around like a roaring lion looking for someone to devour."* 1 Peter 5:8 NIV

And Satan's objective is not just to try to fool you. No, he's trying to kill you spiritually for all eternity. The stakes don't get any higher than that for anyone. Here is God's description, comparing Satan to a thief – a thief that is stealing life and not material possessions:

"The thief comes only to steal and kill and destroy; I have come that they may have life, and have it to the full." John 10:10 NIV

Just as we may not see God's grace in our lives, Satan doesn't show himself as this big threat to us that would cause us to instantly reject his ultimate objective. No, he knows he can deceive us by disguising himself and those who knowingly and unknowingly work on his behalf. Once again, God warns us about Satan's tactics:

"...deceitful workmen, masquerading as apostles of Christ. And no wonder, for Satan himself masquerades as an angel of light. It is not surprising, then, if his servants masquerade as servants of righteousness." 2 Cor 11:14-15 NIV

If nothing else, we owe it to ourselves to be aware that we are Satan's target – we have, so to speak, a price on our souls.

What Are You Doing To Stay Out Of Hell?

Or are you rethinking your position? It's not too late at this point to change. You reading this book is no accident. God knew you would be reading it. You can no longer claim ignorance when it comes to the subject of Hell. It has now been recorded in God's Books as a testimony that you have been warned and given the opportunity to change your eternal destiny.

Just as there is only one way to get to Heaven, there is only one way to avoid going to the Lake of Burning Sulfur. Some people will still deny the reality of Hell, even after reading what God tells us. Are you one of those people? Will you end up like the rich man and have the regrets he had? Don't wait until you end up in Hell, wishing both that you had listened, and that you could try to warn others you know away from ending up in the same place. God is doing everything to make sure this fate is no surprise. Let's re-read what the rich man said:

"... 'Then let me ask you, Father: Send him to the house of my father where I have five brothers, so he can tell them the score and warn them so they won't end up here in this place of torment.' Abraham answered, 'They have Moses and the Prophets to tell them the score. Let them listen to them.' 'I know, Father Abraham,' he said, 'but they're not listening. If someone came back to them from the dead, they would change their ways.' Abraham replied, 'If they won't listen to Moses and the Prophets, they're not going to be convinced by someone who rises from the dead.'" Luke 16:27-31 The Message*

Jesus did come, died and rose again. This is the proof, the evidence; God has given us to validate the reality of this message.

For those of you who have already been reconciled to God, take this message to heart and realize that if you don't do your best to help the people in your life escape this fate, you are lacking love. It was the love of others that saved you from this devastating fate.

Chapter 9

What Now?

At this point, either you chose to accept God's gift of eternal life or elected not to respond - rejected it. In either case, your life will never be the same. You may be asking "How so?" It is more obvious to those of you who are now experiencing a personal relationship with God, as there is an undeniable sense of *knowing* that you are indeed different. The majority of this chapter is addressed to you so you will better understand just how your life will change. The first part of this chapter is for those of you who have chosen not to respond to God's invitation to spend eternity with Him. There is no way to over-emphasize that it is critical for you to revisit that choice before putting this book on the shelf – staying your course is an eternal decision.

For Those Who Are Still Not Sure or Reject God's Gift of Eternal Life

You have now heard the good news that Heaven is where God wants you to spend eternity with Him, and making the way for anyone to enter in without cost. The choice you are making at this point is to remain completely separated from God for all eternity. You are definitely without excuse – the excuse of "I never knew!" The choice you are making has come after being totally informed of the consequences of that decision – that if you do not change your heart, you will be thrown into the Lake of Fire with everyone else who made the same choice.

God is being patient with you, as you still have the opportunity to change your heart. Just how long He will be patient, no one knows, because no one is promised tomorrow. In essence, postponing your decision, thinking you can wait until "one minute before midnight," could be the biggest mistake of your life.

It would be worth your while to re-read the last part of the account of the rich man that you should be familiar with by now. He regretted his decision and was desperately trying to warn his family not to make the same mistake – he knew his fate was sealed. God gave the rich man his opportunity to choose differently, and it is now your opportunity.

It is imperative that you remember that this is not strictly a mechanical act. This is a matter of the heart, and it's only through the condition of your heart that you can genuinely accept God's gift. God will not be fooled or mocked. He knows everything, including your motives, the sincerity of your actions.

God said that His Kingdom belonged to people who are childlike in heart. Not childish, but childlike. What He is saying is you must have the demeanor of a child when you approach God to accept His gift of everlasting life – humble, teachable, vulnerable and trusting.

God loves you no matter what you may have done. His love for you is unwavering and is greater than any wrong you may have committed. He will continue to try to get your attention through the circumstances of your life, and through people who will cross your path. They may already be there – look around, you will find them.

There is nothing more important for you to do than to take the time right now to reflect on this gift God is placing before you. This may not be your last opportunity, but then again, it could be. Are you willing to risk that? Cry out to God, He will reveal Himself to you if you are sincerely seeking Him. You have everything to gain and nothing to lose.

For Those Who Have Accepted God's Gift of Eternal Life

Once again, welcome to God's family! The day you made your peace with God and entered into His Kingdom marks the beginning of your life for the rest of eternity. If you haven't already done so, mark the date you made your peace with God on your calendar. You have a new beginning in God's Kingdom as a member of His family, with all the benefits, privileges and responsibilities. One of the biggest benefits is that all your past mistakes have been completely erased. God cast those sins into the sea of forgetfulness and will never hold them against you – ever! The biggest privilege is that God is giving you direct access to Him. He is also equipping you with the power and authority that comes with being a child of the King of kings.

"Where do I go from here? What's next? How is my life going to change?" These may be some of the questions you are asking yourself. The answer to all your questions are encompassed in the two commandments Jesus gave us. It's that simple – but it may not always be easy. These two commandments capture all other guidelines God could give us, that help us live our lives to the fullest and the way He intended. Everything you do in life from now on should be done with these two commandments in mind. If there is anything in your life that you do that does not keep these commandments, you need to rethink what you are doing. Here are those two commandments again:

The first and greatest of the two commandments has to do with your relationship with God:

"Love the Lord your God with all your heart and with all your soul and with all your mind." Matthew 22:37 NIV

The second commandment has everything to do with your relationship with others:

"Love your neighbor as yourself." Matthew 22:39 NIV

Keeping these two commandments is the foundation of God's plan for your life. It touches every part of your life every day.

The rest of this chapter will only scratch the surface of how you need to develop your relationship with God. It may take you years to understand what God has for you to do, but just like it took time for our bodies to mature into adulthood, it will take time to mature as a member of God's family. Two of the most important things to realize about being in God's family are that:

1. You were just born spiritually – which means you are a babe in Christ (no matter what your age), making you not only anxious to "get started," but also vulnerable to those who are less than thrilled with your decision; and,
2. You need spiritual food to grow strong in your faith. Since you are a member of God's family – it means you need to get with other members of the family who can guide you and help you grow. Get plugged into the family as soon as possible!

Babies need to eat regularly because their bodies are growing very rapidly. That holds true at the spiritual level as well. God tells us we need to feed off of His Word by reading the Bible:

"Man does not live on bread alone, but on every word that comes from the mouth of God." Matthew 4:4 NIV

As you spend time reading, you will sense yourself getting stronger each day. You may already be reading regularly. What's so beautiful about this is you can't "over eat" when it comes to this food! It will renew your mind and your thinking, and change your life.

Another benefit of being in God's family is that He has given us several key promises that we can count on to help us every day. Memorize them, as you will want to remember them when your circumstances challenge you to the point of doubting if God is in your circumstances. These promises will get you through. They reassure us that God is in complete control of every situation, even if we can't see what He is doing. They will also give you His peace, a real sense of security, strength, and courage in everything you do. Here are some of those promises:

1. You are never alone. One of the best parts of being a member of God's family is that God promises He will always be with you, no matter what you are going through and no matter where you are:

"... the Lord your God will go with you. He will not leave you or forget you." Deuteronomy 31:6 NCV

2. God is just getting started with you. As any good parent would, He will guide you daily as you grow. He will do His part of building the relationship:

"... God who started this great work in you would keep at it and bring it to a flourishing finish on the very day Christ Jesus appears." Philippians 1:6 The Message

3. To let you know just how much He has been thinking about you and looking forward to having you as one of His children, He tells you that He has a plan for your life:

"I say this because I know what I am planning for you," says the Lord. "I have good plans for you, not plans to hurt you. I will give you hope and a good future. Then you will call my name. You will come to me and pray to me, and I will listen to you. You will search for me. And when you search for me with all your heart, you will find me!" Jeremiah 29:11-13 NCV

4. You will never face a situation that God has not equipped you to handle, even if you think you are facing the impossible. He knows your limits and will never give you more than you can handle, and He always provides a way out:

"No test or temptation that comes your way is beyond the course of what others have had to face. All you need to remember is that God will never let you down; he'll never let you be pushed past your limit; he'll always be there to help you come through it." 1 Corinthians 10:13 The Message

5. The closer we draw close to God by spending time alone with Him, the closer He will come to us. The less "distance" there is between you and God, the stronger you will become:

"Come near to God and he will come near to you." James 4:8 NIV

There are literally hundreds of promises scattered throughout the Bible. God is bigger and better than what we can understand and take in. That's probably one of the reasons we have all of eternity to spend with Him. It will take that and then some to get to know Him completely, and then we will fall short even then!

Let's see what we can do to grow, mature and find out what God has planned for you by applying our lives to the two commandments.

Love God:

You now have a personal relationship with God. The gap between you and God has been bridged. That means you can start building your relationship with Him right now and continue forever – you're the only one who can ever stop that.

Being God's child has benefits beyond what can be put into words. God is love, so the more you get to know Him, the more you will understand Him and experience the true meaning of love. It is dramatically different from what most people think before they have a personal relationship with God.

When you love people, you love spending time with them. The more you love them, the more time you want to spend with them and include them in everything you do. Have you ever been in love, found your "soul mate?" Your every thought, all your life plans include them. You just can't wait to be with them. It should be the same with God, only even more so. Don't limit your time with Him or exclude Him from any part of your life because there are things you may think He will not be interested in. He knows everything about you and wants to be there for you every moment of your life. Since God is perfect, He is the perfect partner and will always be faithful, no matter what. The more time you spend with God, the more you will realize just how much He loves you.

What do you do when spending time with God? It's once again rather simple. First, set a time when you make it exclusively the two of you – time alone. When you get together, have a conversation – that means you should be talking *and* listening. That's what people refer to as prayer – it's having a conversation with God. There is a wise saying: "We have two ears and one mouth, so we should be listening twice as much as we talk." There are times when we need to be both quiet and still when we spend time with God. He tells us that this is one of the best times to get to know Him – it's when we listen:

"...be still, and know that I am God." Ps 46:10 NIV

Another benefit you have as God's child is you have immediate access to Him – all the time! You don't have to go through anyone else, make an appointment with a secretary. There is never a busy signal, you never have to leave a message or wait for Him to get back to you, and there is no cost for the time you spend when the two of you are talking. The more time you spend with God, the deeper your relationship will be. Your confidence in approaching Him will grow. God tells us that is the way He intended it to be:

"Let us, then, feel very sure that we can come before God's throne where there is grace. There we can receive mercy and grace to help us when we need it." Heb 4:16 NCV

Most of us, however, when we spend time with God, make it only a time when we ask for things we want. That should be only a small part of our time together. It is more appropriate and balanced when we start by thanking Him for all He has done, is doing, and is about to do in our lives and the lives of those we love and care about. It doesn't take long when we look around us to see His "hand" in our lives. He is in the details as much as He is doing the big things. The Psalms are filled with praise and thanksgiving prayers. They will give you a head start on what and how to thank and praise Him.

What should our focus be when we pray to God? The focus should center on what God wants you to do today. He will show you His plan for you, and anything that would help you do that with excellence. Sometimes when God does not seem to answer our request, it's for a good reason. One of them is when our motives are self-centered:

"When you ask, you do not receive, because you ask with wrong motives, that you may spend what you get on your pleasures." James 4:3 NIV

When we do ask God for things with the right motives, remember God knows the best way to bring that about and when to provide. The timing of the answer is one of the hardest things for us to accept. A lot of times the "delay" is because God is waiting for the best opportunity, one that will benefit as many people as possible. Be honest and direct when you ask, and trust that He knows how to answer at the right time:

"Don't bargain with God. Be direct. Ask for what you need. This isn't a cat-and-mouse, hide-and-seek game we're in. If your child asks for bread, do you trick him with sawdust? If he asks for fish, do you scare him with a live snake on his plate? As bad as you are, you wouldn't think of such a thing. You're at least decent to your own children. So don't you think the God who conceived you in love will be even better?" Matthew 7:7-11 The Message

Trust God. He will answer your prayer:

"...if you have faith and do not doubt, ... If you believe, you will receive whatever you ask for in prayer." Matt 21:21-22 NIV

Something else that is an essential part of who you are as God's child, you will find yourself wanting to worship Him. Worship comes in many forms, but one of the main ways is expressing ourselves in the form of singing. There are literally thousands of songs out today that will help you. There are different styles of music – the best ones are the ones that draw you closer to God, that reflect His character and deepen your relationship with Him. Ask another member of God's family where you can get these CDs. If you have access to the Internet, search for "Christian Music." Many sites let you listen to the songs online before you buy. Most communities have radio stations that have both music and teachers. There are also thousands of songs that help us reflect on our walk with God. Check those out too.

You are not perfect yet. None of us are. Perfection will come when we get to Heaven, and only then. Even though God wiped our slates completely clean of all our past sins, we will fall short again. When we do, we will find that God is still in the forgiving business, but we must come to God immediately and confess it. Then we will see:

"God is faithful and reliable. If we confess our sins, he forgives them and cleanses us from everything we've done wrong." 1 John 1:9 NIV

Psalm 51 gives us insight into how our sins move us away from God, seriously affecting our relationship with Him. As we mature, our life's profile of sinning should reflect a decrease in the frequency and severity of these offences against God. We should be getting better and stronger, learning from our mistakes.

You can never exhaust the possibilities of how to develop your relationship with God. We will discover each day just how true this is if we take the time to meet with Him. Before closing this part about loving God, let's read what the apostle Paul prayed for his friends – something we can pray ourselves:

> *"For this reason I kneel before the Father, from whom his whole family in heaven and on earth derives its name. I pray that out of his glorious riches he may strengthen you with power through his Spirit in your inner being, so that Christ may dwell in your hearts through faith. And I pray that you, being rooted and established in love, may have power, together with all the saints, to grasp how wide and long and high and deep is the love of Christ, and to know this love that surpasses knowledge — that you may be filled to the measure of all the fullness of God." Ephesians 3:14-19 NIV*

Love Your Neighbor

Loving God is easier than loving your neighbor. God is perfect and your neighbor is not – and you are someone's neighbor, making you less than perfect. When God refers to your neighbor, He is not simply talking about the people who live next door to you. Your neighbor is everyone who touches your life – family members, co-workers/fellow students, friends and neighbors. Our motivation to love our neighbor needs to be rooted in our love for God, otherwise we will fail miserably. Face it, even the ones we love the most are tough to love at times. So just how can we best love the people who are infinitely more challenging? Ask God for wisdom and realize that there is a reward for loving people outside your "inner circle:"

> *"If you love only the people who love you, you will get no reward. Even the tax collectors do that. And if you are nice only to your friends, you are no better than other people. Even those who don't know God are nice to their friends." Matthew 5:46-48 NCV*

And speaking of rewards, we are in a position with God now so that when we are motivated by our love for God, He will reward us. Some of those rewards even show up down here:

"...receive many times as much in this age and, in the age to come" Luke 18:30 NIV

These rewards become a part of our inheritance. "Did you say inheritance?" Absolutely!

"Come, you who are blessed by my Father; take your inheritance, the kingdom prepared for you since the creation of the world. For I was hungry and you gave me something to eat, I was thirsty and you gave me something to drink, I was a stranger and you invited me in, I needed clothes and you clothed me, I was sick and you looked after me, I was in prison and you came to visit me." Matt 25:34-36 NIV

But notice the motive when these things were done. It was so motivated by the love of God that they needed to be reminded about what they had done:

"Lord, when did we see you hungry and feed you, or thirsty and give you something to drink? When did we see you a stranger and invite you in, or needing clothes and clothe you? When did we see you sick or in prison and go to visit you?" [God] will reply, "I tell you the truth, whatever you did for one of the least of these brothers of mine, you did for me." Matthew 25:37-40 NIV

So if we set out deliberately to just add to our inheritance, there won't be much there, since we are motivated for selfish reasons. You get the drift. Here is one other way in which God gives us the opportunity to show our love to our neighbor:

"Suppose someone has enough to live and sees a brother or sister in need, but does not help. Then God's love is not

living in that person. My children, we should love people not only with words and talk, but by our actions and true caring." 1 John 3:17-18 NCV

There is much more God wants you to do, now that you are a member of His family. He wants you to spend time with the other members of the family so you can grow together in your relationship with God:

"...even though we are many individuals, Christ makes us one body and individuals who are connected to each other. God in his kindness gave each of us different gifts." Romans 12:5-6 NIV

Family in God's Kingdom has a stronger bond than anything that exists in the natural family. And when we get together with other members of God's family, we participate in activities that will help each other in our relationship with God and with each other:

"They spent their time learning the apostles' teaching, sharing, breaking bread, and praying together." Acts 2:42 NCV

This gathering should be in a church setting. You need to be careful that you choose wisely on which church, because there are "Christian" churches out there that have the label but not the right teachings. Make sure they teach and believe the following as the foundation of everything they do:

1. There is only one God, made up of Father, Son and Holy Spirit; three in one, all equally God – the trinity.
2. That the Son is Jesus the Christ – Emmanuel - God with us. That:
    a) Jesus really died - that His crucifixion was a genuine historical event;
    b) Jesus was buried - a real human body being laid in an actual grave;

c) Jesus was raised from the dead; and,
   d) Jesus will come again to take His sheep to be with Him in Heaven for all eternity.
3. The Bible is God's Word: perfect in every way - that is, without error or contradiction.

Ask and look for God to give you a peace about where you should be. Seek good counsel from someone you trust who already has a relationship with God through Jesus.

As mentioned above, no one in God's family is perfect. There will be times when we will be challenged by these imperfections, to the point where we find ourselves needing to forgive one another - sometimes over and again. The question we may ask ourselves in these instances is: "How many times do I forgive?" As usual, God has an answer:

"Lord, when my fellow believer sins against me, how many times must I forgive him? Should I forgive him as many as seven times?" Jesus answered, "I tell you, you must forgive him more than seven times. You must forgive him even if he wrongs you seventy times seven." Matthew 18:21-22 NCV

When you are having a hard time forgiving, remember how God forgave you. It's the least we can do in return to forgive others.

Make it a point to read your Bible every day. It has the answers to all the questions you may have about your life. Just as is so typical of God, in the center of the Bible are two books that contain incredible wisdom that will make our lives as full as can be while down here on Earth. Those books are Psalms and Proverbs. Since many people don't know where to start reading in the Bible, God has made these two books fit our lives rather nicely. There are 31 chapters of proverbs, one for each day of the month – kind of like your spiritual vitamin. Then there are 150 Psalms, enough for 5 a day – these are the power bars to propel us into the day.

Dedicate each day to Him. Make it a point when you have your time alone with God that you think about and plan your day, making sure He would endorse and approve what you do. God does not want us to react to the circumstances in our lives, He wants us to be constantly alert to each opportunity to grow our relationship with Him and love our neighbor.

As you can see what you do there is a lot to learn. Be patient but deliberate; keep a steady pace instead of trying to do it all at once. We don't know how long we have down here what you do but whatever time that is what you do we need it to be the dominant relationship in our lives. There are hundreds of books that can help you with your walk with the Lord, but only one that is always right – the Bible. Some have referred to it as His love letters to us.

Printed in the United States
134717LV00002BA/32/P